CHAMPIONS!

Sheffield United's Championship Triumph 1897–98

CHAMPIONS!

Sheffield United's Championship Triumph 1897–98

First published in Great Britain in 2007 by
The Breedon Books Publishing Company Limited,
3 The Parker Centre, Derby, DE21 4SZ.

This paperback edition published in Great Britain in 2014
by DB Publishing, an imprint of JMD Media Ltd

ACKNOWLEDGEMENTS

The author would like to express his thanks to the following: Andy Pack at Sheffield
United, for the support and assistance he has given towards the project; Denis
Clarebrough, for supplying all the photographs, reading the manuscript and for
contributing his pertinent queries and suggestions; the SUFC Hall of Fame, for
allowing access to the programmes, and the staff at the local studies section of
Sheffield's Central Reference Library. Most of all I would like to thank my wife
Doreen for her patience and understanding during the research and writing of this
book and her encouragement to get the final product published.

ISBN 978-1-78091-442-8

CONTENTS

INTRODUCTORY NOTES

'Blades'

At the end of the 19th century it was common for journalists and supporters, both in Sheffield and elsewhere, to refer to any football team that came from the city as 'Blades' or 'Cutlers'– an obvious association with Sheffield's worldwide reputation for producing fine quality cutlery. Thus, neither United nor Wednesday had a single readily identifiable nickname during the period covered by the book. In fact, the *Independent's* headline for Wednesday's defeat by Sunderland in their opening fixture of the 1897–98 season proclaimed 'The "Blades" Beaten'. Wednesday would move in 1889 from Olive Grove to a new ground in Owlerton, and it was a corruption of that word and its pronunciation which would eventually lead, some years after, to Wednesday fans gradually adopting the nickname of 'Owls'. This meant that United then gradually became the only Sheffield club referred to as Blades. In terms of historical accuracy, I have therefore referred to the team as United throughout the 1897–98 campaign.

Team Formations

The standard line up and numbering for all teams in this period was:

1.
Goalkeeper

2.   3.
Right-back   Left-back

4.   5.   6.
Right-half   Centre-half   Left-half

7.   8.   9.   10.   11.
Outside-right/   Inside-right   Centre-forward   Inside-left   Outside-left/
Right-wing   Left-wing

Each team had two full-backs, three half-backs and five forwards. Although having a good defence was very important, teams and their supporters expected to place the main emphasis on attack wherever possible.

No Substitutes

Substitutions were not introduced until the 1965–66 season, a long time after United's Championship success. Consequently, in many of their games United or their opponents were reduced to fewer than 11 players, when serious injuries forced men from the field. Frequently players would return to the fray as limping 'passengers', of very little use to their team. Most notable in the 1897–98 season was Ralph Gaudie's return to the field of play at Villa Park, after a collision displaced the cartilage in his nose and he was suffering severe pain. At the final whistle he was said to have collapsed, but presumably content that he had not let the side down.

The League Table: Goal Average

It was not until the 1976–77 season that the Football League decided to separate teams on the same points by goal difference rather than goal average. Whereas goal difference – the difference between the goals a team scored and concedes – is easy to work out, goal average is a little more difficult. It is found by dividing the goals scored by the goals conceded, a result which could go to several decimal places. It is perhaps surprising that this method lasted for so long. It was eventually changed in the belief that the system of goal difference would put more emphasis on attacking play, following the heavier emphasis on defence that had developed in the 1960s.

'Fans'/Travelling Supporters

Going back to the later 1890s, it is perhaps surprising to the modern supporter how far we can readily identify our Victorian counterparts as similar to ourselves in the way they passionately followed their teams. Although established less than 10 years, United already had a very loyal following and the club merchandisers, Cole Brothers, had a nice line in club scarves, ties and other articles. The Lane crowd, like those throughout the League, were vocal and partisan. Like today, they roundly booed the referees when they believed them to be incompetent – only towards the home side, of course – and gave a rough ride to players from the opposition who aroused their anger. Although condemning these actions as 'unsportsmanlike', the Football League authorities and directors of some other clubs proved more tolerant of spectators encroaching on to the pitch during the course of play than their modern counterparts today. Although there is little evidence of this problem occurring at Bramall Lane during the period, it did happen elsewhere. It seems that when it did, it was regarded as an example of the over-exuberance displayed by unrefined and passionate

NOTTS. FOREST.

RIGHT WING.   *Goal :*   LEFT WING.

Allsop.

Backs :

Ritchie.   Scott.

Half-Backs :

Forman.   McPherson.   Wragg.

Forwards :

McInnes.   Richards.   Benbow.   Capes.   Spouncer.

Referee :—Mr. J. LEWIS.

Forwards :

Turner.   Stevens   Farrell.   Buchanan.   Brown
(or Keay).   (or Keay).

Half-Backs :

Petrie.   Chadwick.   Meston.

Backs :

Haynes.   Nichol.

Goal :

LEFT WING.   Clawley.   RIGHT WING.

SOUTHAMPTON.

Nottingham Forest and Southampton line up against each other in the FA Cup semi-final at Bramall Lane, 1898.

working-class supporters. It was felt that such actions did not carry with them any malicious intent. During the 1897–98 season, United's committee do not seem to have complained about Everton's supporters throwing stones at goalkeeper Bill Foulke at Goodison Park. However, they did lodge an official protest with the League against Sunderland, who had, due to the presence of a very large crowd, permitted supporters to stand along the touchlines on all four sides of the ground. A number of these spectators had come on to the pitch several times during the game, and the United committee felt that there had been serious intimidation of their players. Unfortunately, the League saw fit to dismiss United's protests with the result that the Sunderland victory stood. Trouble between supporters was rare, although Sheffield derbies led to rising temperatures both on and off the pitch and bystanders would sometimes have to placate those who became too heated, often due to the effects of too much alcohol.

Of greatest interest is the discovery of the large away following that United, even in 1897–98, took to many of their fixtures. The assumption is generally made that except for the odd key game – normally cup semis or finals – away support on a regular basis did not occur until the 1960s, with the emergence of affluent older teenagers. Cheap day excursions by train were already well established before the formation of the Football League, and they allowed even the working classes to go on day visits to the country or seaside. With the great public interest aroused by a competitive Football League, big games started to attract spectators from not only the away teams but also football lovers generally. It had in fact been the choice of Bramall Lane for the FA Cup semi-final of 16 March 1889, between Preston North End and West Bromwich Albion, that had awakened the Sheffield United Ground Committee, also known as the Sheffield United Cricket Club, to the massive interest in football. This persuaded them to start their own football club, which would be essentially professional, but would also include the best local amateur players, to generate income at Bramall Lane over the winter months. A paid attendance of 22,688 – the largest to date for a semi-final tie with thousands turned away – came from Preston, the West Midlands, Sheffield and elsewhere. With such interest in football, the railway companies quickly spotted the potential and offered day excursions to Sheffield supporters for many away fixtures. United regularly took a large following to Nottingham, to play both Forest and Notts County, and in 1897–98 there were particularly large turnouts for the key games at Everton, Aston Villa and Bolton. Away days, as now, were clearly seen as fun days out and, as described in the match

The United team that played against Stoke City, 28 September 1895. Back row, left to right: Waller (trainer), Whitham, Foulke, Docherty, Cain. Middle row: Yates, Hammond, Needham, Hill, Watson. Front row: Thickett, Howell.

commentaries, saw cheerful fans singing their way to and from the ground and loudly backing their team during the game. The players were early celebrities. They were given nicknames by the fans, who during 1897–98 were often present at the railway station to greet their returning heroes. Yet it has to be remembered that then, as now, the fans demanded effort and skill in return, and the players had to endure a particularly trying period at Bramall Lane following the anger and disappointment of their FA Cup replay defeat to Burslem Port Vale.

The Sheffield Newspapers

The two key newspapers used to compile details on United's games and club developments during the 1897–98 season are *The Sheffield Daily Telegraph* and *The Sheffield and Rotherham Independent*. I have referred to them as the '*Independent*' and the '*Telegraph*'. The key football commentators, writing under pseudonyms, were, 'Looker-On' in the *Telegraph* and 'Centre-Forward' in the *Independent*. Excerpts, where appropriate, have been taken from other national sporting and news publications. Football had indeed become a very important part of news reporting by this time.

The Official Sheffield United Club Programme

1897–98 was a landmark season in that it saw the publication of the club's first ever official programme, replacing the scorecards produced by the legendary Sheffield printer Billy Whitham. Importantly, the programme gave the football committee a medium through which they could communicate to the supporters. This is most useful to the historian as it gives an insight into their views on events and developments throughout the season. I have, therefore, taken the comments and analysis in the programme as a reflection of the committee's views on the performances in matches throughout the Championship campaign.

The Football Committee: Tactics and Team Selection

In the first decade of United's existence, the United team was managed by the football committee, aided by the club secretary John Wostinholm and his assistant Henry Herbert Stones. First-team trainer George Waller, his assistant Jack Housley and the team captains advised them on who to select. In the Championship season it is difficult to know exactly who had the biggest influence over training, tactics and selection. Clearly, though, Waller and captain Ernest Needham were all

John Wostinholm.

exceptionally knowledgeable and experienced, and so they probably shared the responsibility equally between them. However, Fred Spiksley, the legendary Wednesday and England winger of the period, believed that the ideas behind United's new style of play for the 1897–98 season, 'long swinging passes from the centre to the outside forwards and wide passing from the halves, backed up with tremendous dash and strength', were most probably devised by Needham, whom he considered a great tactician.

The 1896–97 season

Prior to United's Championship season, the club had finished runners-up in the League to Aston Villa and had declared a profit on the football side of the club of £1,066. It was a good achievement, but satisfaction was tempered by the knowledge that they had finished 11 points adrift of the champions – the result of two identifiable problems. Firstly, United's performances at home had been poor. While the team had been excellent on the road, having won seven, drawn six and lost two, at home they had won six, drawn four and lost five, and went three months between September and December without a home League win. Secondly, the team had not found a successful forward line, and especially a free scoring centre-forward to replace Harry Hammond, who was in his final season with the club.

What the real positive of the 1896–97 season had been, though, was the defensive strength of the team. United had conceded just 29 goals, making them the best in the League, and it was this that would provide the foundation for the success of the following season. The players were all in place: Foulke in goal; Thickett and Cain as full-backs; Morren, Needham and Howell filling the half-back positions. Percy M. Young, in his book *Football in Sheffield*, assessing their importance, wrote:

'The United were a fine side, with what was acknowledged to be the best defence in the kingdom – the half-back line deserving to rank among the best of all time; adaptable and quick to summarise the strengths and weaknesses of any opposition. Needham, as captain, was a great general.'

THE PLAYERS

Note: Given the gaps in available records from the time, the information given is correct to the best of my knowledge. Readers will be able to assess the abilities of the players from the match reports and analysis of the 1897–98 season.

The following players represented United in League games in the Championship season of 1897–98.
*Height/weight/trades as given by the club in 1897–98.
Height/weight – Burslem Port Vale programme 29 January 1898.
Trades – Notts County programme 4 December 1897.
In this period boys left school at 11 years old so therefore worked before becoming professionals.

John Almond

Date of Birth:	6 January 1876
Born:	Darlington
Height:	5ft 11in
Weight:	11st 6lb
Trade/occupation:	Clerk
Position:	Centre/inside-forward
League goals:	7
League appearances:	20

Was signed at the start of the 1896–97 season, having played for Bishop Auckland and Darlington. Made his League debut at home to Sunderland on 19 September 1896, scoring in a 3–0 win.

Walter Bennett

Date of Birth:	1874
Born:	Mexborough
Height:	5ft 8in
Weight:	12st 4lb
Trade/occupation:	Glass bottle blower
Position:	Outside-right
League goals:	12 (top scorer)
League appearances:	26

Walter Bennett.

A right-winger from Mexborough, Bennett had impressed many watching scouts and reporters with his ability to cross the ball accurately and cut inside and shoot with real power. At the end of 1895 United moved to sign him, for a reported fee of £40, although some sources say £10. Bennett made his League debut against West Bromwich in a 1–0 away defeat on 22 February 1896. Big things were expected of him given that he had scored 168 goals in two seasons for Mexborough in the

Midland League, yet initially he was a disappointment. He was said to be moody and had a serious weight problem. By the start of the 1897–98 season, however, Bennett seemed to have overcome the obstacles to his progress and was to find the consistent form that was to prove so crucial to United's success. Walter's confidence and incisive play gained him the nickname of 'Cocky' from the supporters. It was hated by the United committee, who for years tried to persuade the fans and reporters not to use it. Yet, as Farnsworth notes, 'Remarkably, many supporters never knew he was called Walter.' Bennett won a Championship medal, FA Cup-winners' medal and a runners'-up medal with United. He also represented England twice in 1901, playing against Scotland and Wales. Moving to Bristol City in April 1905, he won a Second Division Championship medal in 1906. Returning to play for Denaby United in 1907, Walter took employment in the pits and was tragically killed in a colliery accident in 1908.

Albert Bradshaw

Date of Birth:	Unknown
Born:	Unknown
Height:	Unknown
Weight:	Unknown
Trade/occupation:	Collier
Position:	Goalkeeper
League goals:	0
League appearances:	1

Signed in 1895, Bradshaw was cover for the great Billy Foulke and consequently found his appearances extremely limited – seven in total – five in the League. He made his League debut at Blackburn in a 1–0 defeat on 25 January 1896. He had been signed from the Eckington Works team and played his last League game at Bolton on 11 March 1899.

John Blair

Date of Birth:	Unknown
Born:	Glasgow
Height:	Unknown
Weight:	Unknown

Trade/occupation: Unknown
Position: Half-back
League goals: 0
League appearances: 1

John Blair was signed prior to the start of the season from Stalybridge. Very little is known of him other than that he made his debut, and only League appearance, deputising for Tommy Morren in the season's opener against Derby on 1 September. Blair departed at the end of the 1897–98 season.

Robert Cain

Date of Birth: 13 February 1966
Born: Slamannen near Glasgow
Height: 5ft 7in
Weight: 12st 10lb
Trade/occupation: Collier
Position: Left-back
League goals: 0
League appearances: 30 (ever present)

Scot Bob Cain was signed from Alliance League side Bootle prior to the 1891–92 season. He made his League debut, along with United – following the club's membership of the newly established Second Division – at home to Lincoln City on 3 September 1892. The 1897–98 season saw the player being awarded a 'benefit' for his excellent service to the club – in fact he had not missed a League game for three seasons. After winning a Championship medal, Bob moved on to Tottenham Hotspur in May 1898.

John Cunningham

Date of Birth: 1879
Born: Glasgow
Height: 5ft 5in
Weight: 11st 3lb
Trade/occupation: Moulder
Position: Inside-left/inside-forward

William Henry Foulke.

League goals: 7
League appearances: 24

Cunningham was signed from Preston prior to the start of the 1897–98 season, where he had found it difficult to graduate from the reserves. He made his League debut at home to Blackburn Rovers on 4 October 1897. At the end of his only season with the Blades, Cunningham moved on to Aston Villa.

William Henry Foulke

Date of Birth: 12 April 1974
Born: Dawley, Shropshire
Height: 6ft 2in
Weight: 18st 7lb
Trade/occupation: Collier
Position: Goalkeeper
League goals: 0
League appearances: 29

Always referred to as Foulkes in contemporary newspaper accounts, Foulke was actually his correct surname and therefore used as such in the later match reports. He was signed in April 1894 from village side Blackwell in Derbyshire. He made his League debut against West Bromwich at Bramall Lane on 1 September 1894. 'Little Willy' soon developed into a larger-than-life character who was also an exceptionally good goalkeeper; the foundation on which United built its excellent defence. His weight when he joined the club was only 12st 5lb, but by 1902 it was 22st 8lb. Nevertheless, his goalkeeping ability remained first-rate throughout. Foulke won a Championship and two FA Cup-winners' (and one losers) medals with United and also represented England against Wales in 1897 and the English League against the Scottish League in 1898 and 1900. At the end of the 1904–05 season, Foulke moved on to Chelsea.

P. Archibald French

Date of Birth: Unknown
Born: Unknown
Height: Unknown

Weight: Unknown
Trade/occupation: Unknown
Position: Inside-forward
League goals: 0
League appearances: 1

French made just one appearance for the club – against Notts County away on 31 January 1898 – when he deputised for Kenny McKay at inside-right. He left the club at the end of the season.

Ralph Gaudie

Date of Birth: July 1874
Born: Guisborough
Height: 5ft 7in
Weight: 11st 2lb
Trade/occupation: Unknown
Position: Centre-forward
League goals: 2
League appearances: 6

Ralph Gaudie was an amateur centre-forward from South Bank, signed for the start of the 1897–98 season. He scored twice on his League debut – at Notts County on New Year's Day 1898. He moved to Aston Villa – where he had impressed everyone by returning to the field with a suspected broken nose in United's crucial fixture there at the end of the season.

George Hedley

Date of Birth: 20 July 1876
Born: South Bank, near Middlesbrough
Height: Unknown
Weight: Unknown
Trade/occupation: Unknown
Position: Centre-forward
League goals: 0
League appearances: 2

George Hedley.

An amateur player originating from South Bank, like Gaudie, George made his League debut against West Bromwich away on 26 March 1898. His potential was almost immediately recognised, and the following season he became the club's first-choice centre-forward. Hedley gained two FA Cup-winners' medals – and one losers – with United and represented England against Ireland and Germany in 1901. George also played for the English against the Scottish League in 1900. At the end of the 1902–03 season Hedley moved on to Southampton.

Harold Howard

Date of Birth:	1871
Born:	Rotherham
Height:	Unknown
Weight:	Unknown
Trade/occupation:	Unknown
Position:	Half-back
League goals:	0
League appearances:	3

Signed in 1894, 'Harry' Howard made his League debut at Everton on 5 October 1895, a season when he made 17 appearances in the League for United. Unable to establish himself as a first-team regular, Howard moved to Small Heath (Birmingham), having played his last game for United in April 1901.

Rab Howell

Date of Birth:	1 October 1867
Born:	Wincobank
Height:	5ft 5½in
Weight:	9st 13lb
Trade/occupation:	Collier
Position:	Right-half
League goals:	0
League appearances:	24

Signed from Rotherham Swifts, he came into United's team at the end of March 1890, during the team's first-ever season. Known as the 'little gypsy', after being born in a caravan in Wincobank Woods, he is the only gypsy to have won a Championship medal. His Football League debut was in United's inaugural season in Division Two, against Lincoln City at home on 3 September 1892. He became a key part of United's famous half-back line. Howell was sold to Liverpool following some disappointing performances – particularly his two own-goals at Sunderland – just before the end of the Championship season. Besides winning a Championship medal with United, Howell represented England against Ireland in 1895, gaining a further cap with Liverpool.

Rab Howell.

Thomas Jenkinson

Date of Birth:	Unknown
Born:	Unknown
Height:	Unknown
Weight:	Unknown
Trade/occupation:	Machinist
Position:	Outside-right
League goals:	0
League appearances:	2

William 'Harry' Johnson.

Jenkinson was signed in May 1895 from Gainsborough Trinity. He made his League debut for United at Blackburn on 20 November 1897 and joined Grimsby Town at the end of the season.

William 'Harry' Johnson

Date of Birth:	March 1876
Born:	Ecclesfield
Height:	5ft 8in
Weight:	11st 0lb
Trade/occupation:	Moulder
Position:	Half-back
League goals:	2
League appearances:	10

William 'Harry' Johnson was signed by United for the 1895–96 season but did not make his League debut until 23 October 1897 at home to Preston. Initially used as cover for United's famous trio of half-backs, he was so impressive that he ended up playing in six out of the last nine League games. The sale of Rab Howell before the end of the season showed the great faith the football committee had in his ability. He was known in Blades history as 'Old Harry', as his son, 'Young Harry', later became the leading scorer in the club's history. Harry had another son, Tom, who also played for United. Harry won a Championship, two Cup-winners' and one Cup runners'-up medal with United. He also represented England six times: against Scotland, Wales and Ireland in 1900 and the same three nations in 1903. He also played for the English against the Scottish League in 1903. Harry retired from playing in April 1909 and joined the training staff at the club.

Neil Logan

Date of Birth:	Unknown
Born:	Burnbank, Scotland
Height:	Unknown
Weight:	Unknown
Trade/occupation:	Collier
Position:	Centre-forward

League goals: 4
League appearances: 5

Logan was signed by United in November 1897, having played for Rutherglen Glenncairn FC. He was said to be 19 years old by the local press and almost six feet in height on his League debut, when he scored two goals at Liverpool on 5 February 1898. At the end of the season Logan moved on to Swindon Town.

Kenneth McKay

Date of Birth: Unknown
Born: Scotland
Height: 5ft 5½in
Weight: 10st 11lb
Trade/occupation: Collier
Position: Inside-right
League goals: 5
League appearances: 25

'Kenny' McKay was signed from Hamilton Academical in January 1897, making his League debut at Bury on 20 March 1897. Not only was he a clever player, but he was also noted for his singing voice – a comment in the club programme describing him as a 'silver toned tenor of no mean order. His "Romany Lass" and "My Hieland Home" is class.' Kenny left the club to join Tottenham Hotspur at the end of the season.

Thomas Morren

Date of Birth: Unknown
Born: Unknown
Height: 5ft 5½in
Weight: 10st 9lb
Trade/occupation: Moulder
Position: Centre-half
League goals: 2
League appearances: 26

'Tom' Morren had captained the Middlesbrough team that won the FA Amateur

Thomas Morren.

Cup in 1895. He signed for United in November 1895 and made his League debut against Burnley, away, on 28 December 1895. It is said that he had refused to sign for United unless they promised to find him work in his former trade. He soon proved to be a crucial part of the United defence and their famous half-back line. At United he won a Championship, FA Cup-winners' and losers' medal. He also represented England against Ireland in 1898. Tommy played his last game for United in April 1903, later retiring.

David Morton

Date of Birth:	Unknown
Born:	Unknown
Height:	Unknown
Weight:	Unknown
Trade/occupation:	Unknown
Position:	Forward
League goals:	0
League appearances:	2

Little is known of Morton. He seems to have played for Millwall previously. He had two games for United but was not a success in the forward line. His League debut was in the opening fixture at home to Derby on 1 September 1897 and his second and final game was away at Wolves on 2 October 1897.

Ernest Needham

Date of Birth:	21 January 1873
Born:	Whittington Moor, Chesterfield
Height:	5ft 5½in
Weight:	11st 3lb
Trade/occupation:	Collier
Position:	Left-half/Utility
League goals:	8
League appearances:	29

'Nudger' Needham joined United from Staveley at the start of the 1891–92 season. His first appearances were on the right wing, until injuries to other players meant he was moved into the half-back line by the end of the season. He made his Football League debut in United's first match at home to Lincoln on 3 September 1892 in the inaugural Division Two season. Nudger gained experience playing alongside the experienced

Ernest Needham.

29

Ernest Needham in his England kit.

Billy Hendry, and when the latter was badly injured on the club's tour of Scotland in January 1895 Needham was handed the captaincy. By this time, Nudger had already made his England debut, against Scotland in April 1894. He became a fixture in the international side and a star player, referred to in the newspapers as the 'Prince of half-backs'. With his excellent behaviour on and off the field, and his thinking approach to the game, he was seen as a great role model for youngsters.

'Nudger' won a Championship, two FA Cup-winners' and one losers' medal with United. He played 16 times for England: 1894, 1895 (Scotland), 1897 (Scotland, Wales, Ireland), 1898 (Scotland, Wales), 1899 (Scotland, Wales, Ireland), 1900 (Scotland, Ireland), 1901 (Scotland, Wales, Ireland), 1902 (Wales). He also played for the English against the Scottish League in 1893, 1894, 1895, 1897, 1898 and 1901 and against the Irish League in 1899, 1900, 1901 and 1904. He played his last League game for United on 30 November 1912 at home to Notts County – although he'd been effectively out of the team since the end of the 1908–09 season. Retiring as a player in April 1913, Nudger later worked for the club in several capacities and acted as a scout.

Alfred Ernest Priest

Date of Birth:	1875
Born:	Darlington
Height:	5ft 8in
Weight:	12st 4lb
Trade/occupation:	Engineer
Position:	Outside-left
League goals:	4
League appearances:	28

'Fred' Priest, a young left-winger from South Bank, was signed after a trial in April 1896. He was a key member of the side from his first full season, 1896–97, and made his League debut at home to Burnley on 5 September 1896, scoring the only goal of the game. Fred won a Championship, two FA Cups and a Cup-losers' medal with United and played once for England in 1900 against Ireland. Fred left the club in December 1905, returning initially to South Bank.

Alfred Ernest Priest.

Harry Thickett

Date of Birth: 28 March 1873
Born: Hexthorpe
Height: 5ft 9½in
Weight: 13st 2lb
Trade/occupation: Brass manufacturer

Position: Right-back

League goals: 0

League appearances: 29

Harry joined the club as an amateur from Hexthorpe Wanderers initially in the 1890–91 season. Making a handful of appearances, he was unable to break into the first team on a regular basis and left to join Rotherham Town in 1892. However, by December 1893 he had impressed United with his development, and they paid a fee of £20 to re-secure his services. Harry made his League debut at home to Everton

Harry Thickett.

on 9 December 1893. By the following season Harry was well established as the club's right-back. Harry won a Championship, two FA Cups and a Cup-losers' medal with United. He represented England twice in 1899, against Scotland and Wales, and the English against the Scottish League in 1898. Harry moved on to play for Bristol City in May 1904, taking over the job of manager later in the following season.

Henry White

Date of Birth:	Unknown
Born:	Unknown
Height:	Unknown
Weight:	Unknown
Trade/occupation:	Unknown
Position:	Centre-forward
League goals:	0
League appearances:	6

White was signed for the start of the 1897–98 season, and the club had hopes that he would develop into a useful centre-forward. He was certainly given a five-game run as the campaign commenced – his debut at home to Derby on 1 September 1897 – and a good opportunity to prove himself. Proving ineffective, he lost his place and moved on to Everton in January 1898.

Michael Whitham

Date of Birth:	6 November 1867
Born:	Ecclesfield
Height:	Unknown
Weight:	Unknown
Trade/occupation:	File Cutter
Position:	Full/half-back
League goals:	0
League appearances:	1

'Mick' Whitham was signed from Rotherham Swifts in February 1890 – United's first season – and quickly established himself as an indispensable member of the

Michael Whitham.

side. An excellent full or half-back, Mick was selected to play for England at left-half against Ireland in March 1892. On 3 September 1892 Mick and United made their debut in the Football League in a home Division Two fixture against Lincoln City. Mick was coming to the end of his playing career when the 1897–98 season came around, and with the excellence of United's defence and the emergence of Harry Johnson as an effective deputy for the half-back line Mick made only one appearance – his last for the club – against Blackburn at Bramall Lane on 4 October 1897. Mick returned to his trade as a file cutter and worked as a trainer at a number of clubs.

WAGES

Figures for the 1896–97 season saw Needham and Foulke as the club's biggest earners on £3 10s 0d a week. In 1897–98 Priest, Morren, Thickett and Cunningham were on £3 a week.

These wages are clearly not of the proportions enjoyed by top Premier League and international players today, but as professional footballers came from the ranks of the working classes they compared very favourably to what their contemporaries were earning. For example, at the start of the 20th century a skilled engineer working in a Manchester engineering works earned £1 15s 6d a week; an engineer's labourer was paid 19s – £1 a week. A bricklayer earned £1 18s a week; his labourer 19s a week (source, *England 1807 – 1914: Ensor*). In a study of poverty in York in 1901, Seebohm Rowntree set the poverty line at £1 1s 8d a week; the basic cost of necessities for a husband, wife and three children. Clearly, then, United's best players were relatively comfortable compared with their contemporaries, but certainly did not have the financial clout to enjoy anything near the standard of living of today's 'stars' – or even average Premier League players.

In 1897–98 retirement from playing meant that players – without today's pensions – had no alternative but to return to the trades they had learned after leaving school. In consequence, the players of 1897–98, and indeed up to the 1960s, were far closer to the communities they represented on the field in their levels of income and lifestyles than their modern 'star' counterparts.

THE 1897–98 SEASON:

MATCH REPORTS AND ANALYSIS

As today, written match reports and analysis by commentators in the media are very much influenced by the attitudes of the individuals providing them. In addition, events happen so quickly on the football field that without the advantage of video replays mistakes can be made on the exact recounting of the details of incidents. The latter is clearly a potential hazard in 1897–98, where such technology was unavailable. Consequently, in producing the details of matches and analyses of the action, I am aware that there may be some discrepancies that arise. However, I have reproduced, as reliably as possible, a 'feel' for the games themselves; excitement where it existed, disappointment when it did not. Importantly, the responses of the reporters, analysts and spectators, along with the club itself, give us an accurate 'feeling' of the times and a fair degree of certainty over the key events and actions of individuals in the matches covered. Hopefully the twists and turns of the season, the highs and lows, will come out in a reading of this record of United's greatest ever achievement, becoming League Champions. Enjoy the season!

MATCH NO. 1

DERBY, HOME, 1 SEPTEMBER 1897

Result: United 2: *Bennett, Needham*
             Derby 1: *J. Goodall (pen)*

Half-time   1–0
Attendance: 2,500

Teams:
United: Foulke, Thickett, Cain, Howell, Blair, Needham, Bennett, Morton,
           White, Almond, Priest.
Derby: Frail, Methven, Leiper, Cox, A. Goodall, Staley, J. Goodall, Bloomer,
           Boag, Maconnachie, McQueen.

Referee: Mr J. West (Lincoln)

The opening of the 1897–98 season, on a Wednesday, saw the introduction of the club's first ever official programme. Not only giving details of the two teams' line-ups, it was also a useful vehicle for the football committee to communicate information to the supporters. The Derby programme set out the club's objectives on the field, the committee boldly declaring 'Ours is to gain the Championship of the League, to win the English Cup, and to be at peace and to work in concord with everyone.'

The increased reliability of communications was shown in the announcement that the scores of all League clubs would be displayed at half and full-time, 10 minutes after the final whistle. It was a clear indication of how quickly the new football competition had aroused the enthusiasm of the public. Supporters of all clubs were eager to monitor the progress of their team and work out their League position relative to others.

The programme noted the promising form of W.H. (Harry) Johnson of the reserves: 'During all United's practises, few men have done better…He will be heard of soon.' The comment was to prove prophetic, but less so in the case of White, who

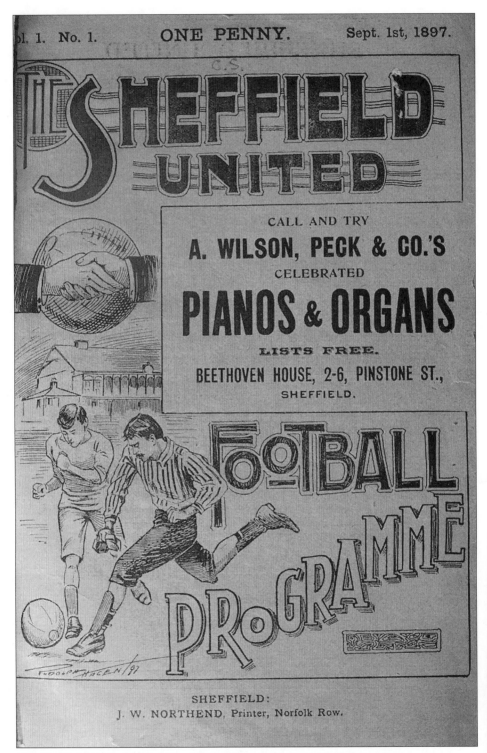

The Sheffield United, Vol. 1 No. 1 from the opening game of the season.

'has framed very well as centre', yet did not prove a success and was soon out of the side. There was also optimism for John Almond, who 'dribbles better than ever and should make Priest a smart partner.'

First half

United had three new players in the team: Blair, Morton and White. Morton was in for Tommy Morren, and the other two were put in hopefully to solve the team's lack of penetration in the forward line. Derby's most notable player was the legendary England forward Steve Bloomer.

The attendance of around 2,500 was disappointing, but this was a result of appalling weather, which continued throughout the game, with torrential rain making it exceptionally difficult for the players.

United won the toss and kicked towards the Shoreham Street end with the advantage of the wind. The opening stages of the game were evenly contested. Foulke made two excellent saves from McQueen and Bloomer, while Frail dived full length to keep out an Almond effort. Misfortune then struck the home side as new man Morton was injured and, with no substitutes, left them with only 10 men as he departed from the field of play. Yet, ironically, it was United who seized the initiative, and on 39 minutes they were a goal up. Bennett received the ball out on the right, eluded the challenge of Methven, cut inside and unleashed a shot across the goal, which went in off the far post. United continued to press but could not add to their tally before the half-time whistle.

Second half

Morton was still not back as the teams returned, and Derby now seemed in a very determined mood, getting on top early and bombarding the United goal. Although Morton finally re-emerged, it was clear that he was not fit and was of very little use for the rest of the game. Derby's pressure finally told as Howell handled the ball in the box and the referee awarded a penalty. Yet luck was not on their side, as the *Independent's* match reports recounts, 'Archie Goodall took and made a wretchedly bad shot, sending the ball yards wide of the goal to the great jubilation of the United players and spectators.'

The game ran freely from this point, the play flowing from end to end, as both sides were hell bent on going all out for goals. Lightning struck twice, however, as another United defender, this time Thickett, handled in the box. Awarded another penalty-kick, this time J. Goodall took it and equalised, making no mistake.

As both sides searched for the winner, the game's major point of controversy occurred. Almond ran through the Rams defence and beat Frail with a shot that seemed clearly to go between the posts and out through the net. The referee's first indication was to point to the centre circle, indicating a goal, but was then persuaded to consult his linesmen, one of whom was the Derby trainer, filling in for an official who had not turned up. The net was not examined and Mr West changed his mind and awarded a goal-kick. The *Telegraph's* reporter claimed to have examined the net later and seen a huge tear through which the ball could have passed. The *Independent's* correspondent concurred that Almond's effort was good. Clearly, the supporters were not happy as the decision was 'loudly hooted'. The issue was to have later ramifications, however, as the League realised the dangers of allowing team representatives to run the line in the new professional age, where the competitive and financial considerations were so great.

Happily for United, circumstances conspired to give them the reward that, on the balance of play, they probably deserved. With a couple of minutes to go, United gained a free-kick for hand-ball, 25 yards out from the Derby goal. Needham struck it and Frail seemed to have it covered, but he fumbled the ball which crossed over the line, giving the home team a 2–1 victory.

Assessments

The teams were well matched, with little to choose between them in terms of ability. However, United made better use of their chances and, perhaps surprisingly, the Derby 'forwards lacked the precision and combination' they had shown in the previous season.

Special mention was made in the *Independent* match report of Foulke: 'as great a goalkeeper as ever and made several brilliant saves early in the game'. 'Looker on' in the *Telegraph* was particularly impressed by 'Almond, who improved almost out of recognition, showed both speed, dash and judgement.'

MATCH NO. 2

PRESTON, AWAY, 4 SEPTEMBER 1897

Result: Preston North End 1: *Stevenson*
United 3: *Bennett, Priest (2)*

Half-time 1–1
Attendance: 4,500, Deepdale

Teams:

United: Foulke, Thickett, Cain, Howell, Morren, Needham, Bennett, McKay, White, Almond, Priest.

Preston: Trainer, Holmes, Dunn, Pratt, Sanders, Drummond, Smith, Hargreaves, Stevenson, Boyd, McLatchie.

Referee: Mr A.J. Barker (Newcastle)

With Tommy Morren back at centre-half for Blair, United had their full and half-back lines, which had been so successful the previous season, back in place. The only other change came at inside-right where Scotsman Kenny McKay came in for the injured Morton.

First half

It had been raining before kick-off but fortunately held off for the duration of the game. United started well. They gained an early corner from which Trainer put a Needham shot over the bar. Bennett was prominent in all the visitors' early attacks; one good run resulting in a shot that hit the post and rebounded to safety. Generally on top, United's defence were almost caught out when a fierce shot by McLatchie was superbly palmed away at full stretch by Foulke, only to fall to Stevenson who, with an empty net, blazed the ball over the bar. United soon regained the ascendancy, and after failing to take several chances went in front with a move that was to become a trademark of their play throughout the season. The ball started with Morren, who sprayed it out to Priest on the left wing. Priest raced down the

43

flank and swung a wide, sweeping pass to Bennett on the opposite side, who smashed the ball past Trainer.

Just before half-time the vulnerability of the narrow lead was displayed, as an uncharacteristic error by Needham let in the Preston forwards and, as the *Independent* recounts, 'Foulke rushed out to save but he went down with Thickett and a couple of Preston forwards, the ball rolling out to Stevenson who easily equalised.'

Second half

Early in the half the visitors were given an excellent chance to regain the lead as Pratt fisted away a cross in the area and a penalty was awarded. Bennett, having a great game, took it, but Trainer saved; Bennett's first penalty miss. The disappointment did not knock United out of their stride, however, and they continued to play the better football. After 65 minutes they had regained the lead with a goal that was a reversal of their first. This time a sweeping pass from Bennett on the right wing to Priest on the left was controlled by the latter and swept fast and low into the Preston net.

Trainer, who was having an excellent game, had no chance with the shot. The Preston custodian, however, continued to keep the visitors at bay with fine saves from White and Almond. When Preston did get forward, they found United's backs and half-backs very difficult to break down.

Near the end of the game, United got their third. From a corner, Bennett crossed into Priest who, for a moment, seemed to have the ball caught under his feet. However, the left-winger recovered and fired the ball past Trainer.

Assessment

'Looker On', in the *Telegraph*, saw the result in rather an amusing fashion, declaring that Preston were not yet match fit or ready for the new season: 'The Prestonians are essentially a 'big' team: when training has been more rigorously attended to, it is certain that form of a more satisfactory nature will result.' Essentially, the Preston team had 'piled on the pounds' during the close-season lay off.

'Centre-forward' in the *Independent* was complimentary about United's efforts. The victory was 'thoroughly well deserved, and the performance was a most meritorious one'. Yet both commentators noted that, although Preston had to thank their 'keeper Trainer for keeping the score down, there was still room for improvement in the United forward line. Early concerns were emerging that the prolific striker the team needed to become serious contenders for honours had not yet been found. White, the present incumbent in the centre-forward berth, was already seen to be coming up short, not prominent enough in the play or showing enough 'dash'.

However, there were other positives, particularly in the form of Walter Bennett. The player had an excellent game and was now fulfilling the great promise that had led to his signing from Mexborough. The key to his improvement was widely believed to be the fact that he had lost two stones since the end of the previous season. He was fitter, faster and now possessed a powerful and lethal shot; he was becoming a key component of the forward line.

Table

		P	W	L	D	Pts
1.	Wolves	2	2	0	0	4
2.	United	2	2	0	0	4
3.	Aston Villa	2	2	0	0	4

Other results

Wolves 3–0 Bury

Villa 4–3 West Brom

MATCH NO. 3

STOKE, HOME, 11 SEPTEMBER 1897

Result: United 4: *Morren, McKay (2) Bennett*
Stoke 3: *Maxwell (2) Thickett (og)*

Half-time 2–2
Attendance: 11,000

Teams:
United: Foulke, Thickett, Cain, Howell, Morren, Needham, Bennett, McKay, White, Almond, Priest.
Stoke: Johnstone, Robertson, Eccles, Ponsonby, Grewer, Murphy, Pugh, J. Hill, T. Hill, Maxwell, Schofield.

Referee: Mr H. Shelton (Nottingham)

Having won the first two games, the club programme made its first assessment of the progress made by the team to date, and it is an early indication of the general feelings held by observers throughout the coming season. United were a 'team' in every sense of the word – no real stars, other than Needham, but a bunch of committed and hard-working players.

'If knock out was the game we should not, for ours it no heavyweight team; it is one of goers…and will do all they can for the club and you.'

Enthusiasm built up from the early victories led to a call for supporters to attend United's next away game at Nottingham Forest. Excursion trains were departing from Sheffield at 1.10pm to return at 8.45pm, for a fare of 2/- (shillings). 'How many of you will go with us to Nottingham? We want a lot' went the request, and it was clear that then, as now, there was a strong rivalry with the City of Nottingham, the 'Club Gossip' page declaring 'come and see us thrash the Forest.'

Certainly, although professional League football was only recently established, all the trappings and paraphernalia of the 'fan' were already well in place. Supporters were informed that a selection of team merchandise, including club ties, scarves etc., was available at the Cole Brothers Store on Fargate.

Of further interest were the nicknames that had been evident for some of United's players among the supporters who had gone to Preston. Almond was referred to as 'the gentleman player', Howell 'the evergreen', Foulke 'Little Willie', Needham 'the Master' and Bennett 'the ex-best shot of the Midland League'.

First half

United were unchanged from the Preston game and expected a tough test from Stoke, who had beaten Notts County and drawn with Liverpool in their first two games. Maxwell had already scored three times and looked the danger man here. The pitch was in good condition and the weather fine, which helped attract a crowd of 11,000.

United kicked-off towards the Bramall Lane end full of optimism, but they were rocked back on their heels after just three minutes as Stoke danger man Maxwell fired home, in off the far post. The disastrous start became even worse on six minutes as a long ball into the United box from the Stoke right was diverted on to his own crossbar by Thickett and into the net.

Yet, as the *Independent* noted, 'instead of being discouraged the United played up with any amount of pluck and dash.' After 20 minutes they had a goal back. Ponsonby fouled Priest, the free-kick was taken and Morren headed in. The game was now full of action. Johnstone saved several shots, while both teams had a goal disallowed for offside, Priest for United and Maxwell for Stoke. After 30 minutes, United's comeback was complete. Eccles mis-kicked a clearance which fell to McKay, who fired in amid 'great cheering'.

It was a game played at a frantic pace, full of 'thrills and spills'. 'Play was very exciting, but not particularly scientific, fierce individual tussles and speedy dashes from end to end, being more in evidence than combination.' (*Independent*) Just before half-time, it seemed United had the lead. A United free-kick was deflected by a Stoke defender, Johnstone seemingly grasping the ball after it had crossed the line. After consulting with his linesmen, however, referee Mr Shelton declared no goal had been scored.

Second half

A minute after the restart United were in front. Almond passed to Priest and the left-winger proceeded to dribble past several opponents before unleashing a shot which Johnstone could only parry. After a goalmouth scramble, the ball eventually fell to Bennett who knocked it home. Stoke attempted to get back into the game by attacking down the flanks. However, they found United full-backs Thickett and Cain in fine form. United were also eager to score another, and a neat run and cross from Bennett was met by Almond who struck the City bar with a thunderous shot.

As play ebbed and flowed, the referee disallowed another two efforts for offside, McKay for United and T. Hill for City, the latter decision being seen as rather contentious.

With Stoke entering the last period desperately pressing for the equaliser, there was always the chance United could catch them on the break. White gave them a warning with a shot against the bar, and with 10 minutes to go Bennett, 'running the leather along in irreproachable style' (*Independent*), broke through the City defence and crossed in from the right. As White and Johnstone challenged for the ball, it ran loose to McKay, who put away his second of the afternoon. It was fortunate United had the two-goal cushion as Maxwell popped up again just before the end to send in a curling shot out of Foulke's reach, to make the score 4–3.

Assessments

United had again shown their character and team spirit, not allowing the early two-goal deficit to put them off their stride. There was another positive display from Bennett, his crossing being especially good. Pleasing too was the way in which the winger had linked up with his inside-right, Kenny McKay. McKay's passing had been good and clever, while Fred Priest had a good game on the left wing.

There were some negative points, however. 'Looker On' in *The Telegraph* remarked on how the two full-backs had been a little erratic at the start – which a team of superior forwards could have exploited further – though acknowledged that both men recovered well. Thickett was praised for 'a lot of splendid work in which his speed was continually to the fore and his overhead kicking [long clearance passing] both clean and vigorous.'

'Looker On' also returned to the key concern he had mentioned after the game at Preston – the absence of a good centre-forward who could convert the excellent chances being created by Bennett and Priest. 'Given a centre-forward as good as the wings, their forward string would be a rare good one.'

Yet for all that, 'Centre-Forward' in the *Independent* noted 'on present form, United will take a lot of beating.'

Table

		P	W	L	D	Pts	
1.	United	3	3	0	0	6	The only unbeaten teams
2.	Aston Villa	3	3	0	0	6	
5.	Sunderland	2	2	0	0	4	

Other results

Notts County 2–3 Aston Villa

MATCH NO. 4

NOTTINGHAM FOREST, AWAY, 18 SEPTEMBER 1897

Result: Forest 1: *Capes*

United 1: *Almond*

Half-time 1–1

Attendance: 8,500, The City Ground

Teams:

United: Foulke, Thickett, Cain, Howell, Morren, Needham, Bennett, McKay, White, Almond, Priest.

Forest: Allsop, Ironmonger, Scott, Frank Foreman, McPherson, Wragg, Fred Foreman, Spencer, Benbow, Richards, Arthur Capes.

Referee: Mr Ramsbottom (Liverpool)

United had always found away fixtures at Forest to be a difficult proposition and, regardless of having a 100 percent record at the City Ground, expected this game to be no different. The game had certainly aroused the interest of United's supporters, and many had responded to the club's call to travel to support the team. Hundreds had gone, the later home match programme against Bury declaring 'Talk about enthusiasm! We never had a trip like that of last Saturday…There were masters and men, lads and ladies…all bent on seeing the match…and we took our bugler too!'

Quite clearly, in these early days, the club had quite a cosmopolitan following, and they were determined to enjoy themselves in the beautiful weather present at the City ground.

First half

For the first period of the game Forest generally played the better football, but after finding good positions, their shooting was wayward. Howell and Needham both had good shots blocked by Forest defenders and a run by Bennett ended in a shot that was headed out from under the bar by Ironmonger.

After 25 minutes, Forest were a goal up, as Capes out on the left fired an excellent shot past Foulke. The goal marked a period of Forest dominance as United struggled to find the form of their previous games. However, on 40 minutes the visitors were level. McKay sent in a cross from the right that was headed home by Almond, his first of the season.

Second half

The game was strongly contested, and Forest were a physically tough but generally fair team. Bennett, having started the half well, was heavily tackled, receiving a nasty thigh injury which effectively meant he was a passenger for the rest of the game. Morren's shin pad was cut 'clean through' following a strong tackle.

With Forest gaining the ascendancy, Foulke made several good saves, but he was thankful for the alertness of the referee when Forest's Scott scored directly from an indirect free-kick and the official disallowed it.

Towards the end, United came back into the game and almost snatched a last-gasp winner. From a corner Howell's powerful shot hit Ironmonger, who was sprawled on the floor, and rebounded to safety.

Assessments

It was generally felt that United had slipped from their impressive standards of recent games. The usually reliable Needham and Howell were seen as being slightly off-form. However, again the team had dug in when the game had become difficult, had secured a draw and could even have won it at the death. Summing up United's performance, *Football World* declared that the team 'showed somewhat a falling off from form previously shown', yet 'possess the ability and courage away from home, which is an important factor in winning championships'.

Table

		P	W	L	D	Pts
1.	Aston Villa	4	4	0	0	8
2.	United	4	3	0	1	7
3.	Derby	4	3	1	0	6

Other results

Villa beat Bury 3–1 to go top – the only team with a 100 percent record.

MATCH NO. 5

BURY, HOME, 25 SEPTEMBER 1897

Result: United 1: *Priest*
                 Bury 1: *Settle*

Half-time   0–1
Attendance: 11,000

Teams:
United: Foulke, Thickett, Cain, Howell, Morren, Needham, Bennett, McKay, White, Almond, Priest.
Bury: Thompson, Darroch, Barbour, Pray, Clegg, Ross, Cust, Settle, Millar, Henderson, Plant.

Referee: Mr J. Grant (Liverpool)

United were again unchanged, while Bury were without their first-choice goalkeeper Montgomery. Thompson was, however, to prove an able deputy. Keen to take advantage of the enthusiasm raised by United's good start, the match programme advertised season tickets at 10/6 for the terrace and 21/- for self and lady to sit in the John Street stand; the same amount secured a reserved seat.

First half

The weather was fine as United, who had lost the toss, kicked-off towards the Bramall Lane end. The game started in competitive fashion with both sides pressing. Foulke comfortably saved long shots by Barbour, Plant and Ross, while Bennett excited the home fans with some clever runs, fine crosses and a long shot that went narrowly wide. Gradually, United were getting on top and from a free-kick, awarded for a trip on White by Pray, almost went ahead. Forty yards out, Needham knocked the ball to Howell, whose shot was only just tipped over the bar by Thompson. Down the flanks, however, Bennett and Priest were finding their respective full-backs – Barbour and Darroch – in fine form and the home side were finding it hard to break down their opponents. In addition, the visitors were mounting some dangerous attacks of their own, and on 40 minutes they took the lead. The ball was moved swiftly from left to right, the Bury inside-right, Settle, shot and Foulkes, though he got his fingers to the ball, was unable to keep it out.

Just before half-time two magnificent long shots by Needham were just kept out by Thompson. Going in a goal down at half-time, United knew they would have a serious battle on their hands in the second half.

Second half

United started in determined mood. Bennett shot just wide; Almond, in the box, fired over when it seemed easier to score; a White long shot hit the bar and McKay shot over from a

An advert for season tickets inside *The Sheffield United* programme.

clear opening. United were proving both profligate and unlucky in front of goal, a state of affairs that continued as a McKay shot again hit the bar and White, put through by Almond, spurned a glorious chance as he missed his kick in front of goal.

Finally, however, the equaliser came. On 75 minutes Bennett crossed from the right and Priest headed in. With an animated crowd behind them, United now pushed on for the winner, pressurising the Bury defence for the last 15 minutes. It almost seemed United had won it as Priest fired in a fierce long-range shot, but it was brilliantly saved by Thompson.

Assessments

Bury had proven to be tough opponents, but the chances had certainly been there for United to win the game. Even though Thompson had performed heroically in the Bury goal, United had hit the woodwork on several occasions and could, therefore, be considered unlucky. The reality was, according to 'Looker On' in the *Telegraph*, that 'the match was…thrown away' – they should have won by three goals. Criticism was now beginning to home in on White – in fact he only made one further appearance for the team – adding to the concerns with United's centre-forward from previous games. 'Looker On' was particularly harsh on White, who, he wrote, did not 'deal with repeated fine centres by both Priest and Bennett' and 'was practically useless throughout the game.'

Table

		P	W	L	D	Pts
1.	United	5	3	0	2	8
2.	Aston Villa	5	4	1	0	8
3.	Derby	5	3	1	1	7

With Aston Villa unexpectedly losing 4–3 to outsiders Blackburn at Ewood Park, United went back to the top of the table on goal average.

MATCH NO. 6

WOLVES, AWAY, 2 OCTOBER 1897

Result: Wolves 1: *McMain*

             United 1: *Almond*

Half-time: 0–0
Attendance: 8,500, Molineux

Teams:

Wolves: Baddeley, Eccles, Blackett, Griffiths, Owen, Fleming, Tonks, McMain, Beats, Wood, Miller.

United: Foulke, Thickett, Cain, Howell, Morren, Needham, Bennett, McKay, Morton, Almond, Priest.

Referee: Mr Kingscott (Derby)

Wolves were in sixth place, having gained five points from their opening five games. They had a settled line up, having fielded the same team since the start of the season.

United had made one key change at centre-forward. Following mounting criticism of White, Morton (who had been injured playing at inside-right in the opening game against Derby) returned to the team to replace him, in the hope that this would give more potency to the attack.

First half

The Wolves team immediately went into their favoured style of play; aggressive, determined challenges with the ball hoisted from back to front as quickly as possible. United found it extremely difficult to adapt to the Wolves tactics and made little progress against their opponents' powerful half-back line, the *Independent* noting that 'one after the other the United men were sent to grass'. Wolves' veteran inside-left, Wood, was prominent in all their attacks, and only a brilliant save by Foulke stopped him putting the home side a goal up before half-time.

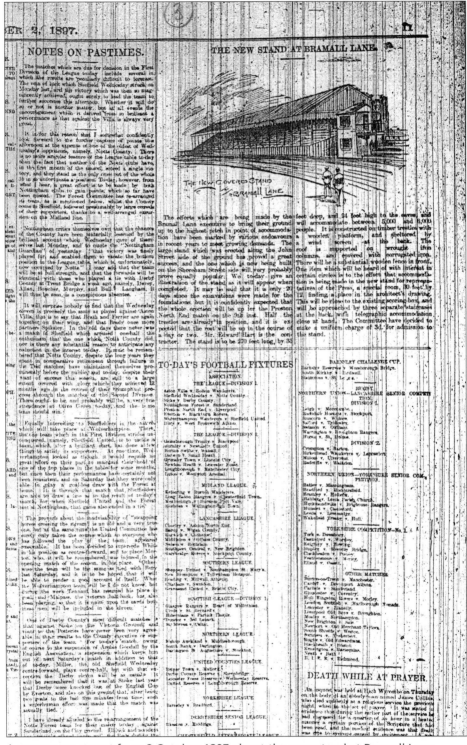

A newspaper report from 2 October 1897 about the new stand at Bramall Lane.

Second half

United had played poorly in the first half but managed to keep parity with their opponents. However, almost immediately after the restart McMain took advantage of slack defensive work to score past Foulke. There followed some intense Wolves pressure, but fortunately the United custodian was able to keep the home team at bay. During this period, United had only one real effort on goal, Needham grazing the bar with a powerful shot. It was the physical strength of Wolves that was continuing to dominate, the visitors seemingly unable to respond. The *Independent* noted that during this passage of play 'The United men appeared somewhat afraid of their burly opponents and did not idle long on the ball as a rule.'

Effectively, Wolves deserved to be well ahead by the mid-point of the half, but fortunately for United luck seemed to be on their side – especially when a corner went clear across their penalty area and two Wolves forwards failed to connect, with what was effectively an open goal. Following this, Thickett fortuitously cleared the ball over his own cross bar, and then Wolves had a goal disallowed as Owen scored directly from an indirect free-kick.

This finally seemed to rouse United into action, and for the last 15 minutes they finally got a grip on the game, as both Bennett and Priest went close. Wolves now seemed to be tiring but still had the strength to flatten both Howell and Thickett – the latter a limping 'passenger' from this point on. But United's new found energy was not to be denied, as a smart downfield run by Bennett ended with the winger playing the ball in to Almond, who smashed a shot high into the roof of the net past Baddeley. According to the *Telegraph*, it was 'a goal as lucky as it appeared brilliant'.

Now very much on top, United passed the ball around well, but there was to be no addition to their score. At the end the initiative was with Wolves, as they forced a corner. However, Foulke, who had had another fine game, showed his great physical strength as he fisted the ball away, halfway down the field.

Assessments

The game had proved very tough for United, and on the balance of play they were somewhat fortunate to have gained a draw. Wolves had certainly been fired up, keen to defeat the League's top club – a situation United would have to get used to dealing with if they had ambitions to maintain their position in the future.

'Looker On' in the *Telegraph* was very critical of United's performance. It was 'A lucky draw.' 'Everything up to the last quarter of an hour of the game pointed to ignominious defeat and all because of the incompetence of their forwards.' The opinion was shared by the club itself, their comment on the game in the Blackburn programme on 4 October 1897 noting '…we got off with a point more than we deserved…our front rank was no use at all till the last quarter of an hour.'

'Centre-forward', in the *Independent*, was not quite so harsh. He actually complimented United's powers of recovery, given that they 'went through a trying ordeal and came out of it with credit.' The 'trying ordeal' referred to the physical nature of the Wolves tactics, a point reflected by the club's own comment that 'though we don't accuse the Wolves of superabundant roughness, they didn't lose anything for lack of energy.'

Clearly there was again disappointment up front, especially at centre-forward, where Morton came in for the same criticism as White and was regarded as a failure – not appearing for the first team again. However, the club were very pleased with the performance of their right full-back: 'Bob Cain played a rare game on Saturday. He was as steady as a rock all through. It was his best game of the present season.'

Table

		P	W	L	D	Pts
1.	Aston Villa	7	5	2	0	10
2.	United	6	3	0	3	9
3.	Derby	6	3	2	1	7
4.	Sunderland	5	3	1	1	7
5.	Stoke	6	3	2	1	7

Other results
Villa 3–2 Bolton
Stoke 2–1 Derby

Aston Villa had lost at Olive Grove to Wednesday on the previous Monday but had then defeated Bolton 3–2 at home to go back to the top.

MATCH No. 7

BLACKBURN ROVERS, HOME, 4 OCTOBER 1897

Result: United 5: *Almond, Bennett, Needham (3, 1 pen)*

Blackburn 2: *Wilkie, Booth*

Half-time: 2–2

Attendance: 8,000

Teams:

United: Foulke, Whitham, Cain, Howell, Morren, Needham, Bennett, McKay, Almond, Cunningham, Priest.

Blackburn: Knowles, Glover, Brandon, Killean, Houlker, Booth, Campbell, Wilkie, Proudfoot, Hulse, Briercliffe.

Referee: Mr T. Armitt (Leek)

With Thickett still injured from the Wolves game, Mick Whittam, who had been with United since their inaugural season, deputised in his final first-team appearance for the side. Up front, the problematic centre-forward shirt was now handed to John Almond with ex-Preston reserve Scotsman John Cunningham brought in to Almond's old position of inside-left. Blackburn had been steadily improving after a poor start to the season. They had beaten Aston Villa and had recently gained a draw against Everton at Goodison Park. Therefore, no one at the Lane was expecting an easy time in this Monday afternoon fixture.

The match programme, meanwhile, congratulated itself on the fact that 1,800 copies had been sold at the recent game against Bury. It seemed to vindicate the club's decision to print its own programme. Other items of news concerned the new stand that was in the process of being constructed at the Shoreham Street End. It was to be 270 feet long and 24 feet high, and the club anticipated that it would be able to accommodate between 5,000 and 6,000 spectators. Notable, too, it was hoped, were the new caps that the players had now been issued with. 'How do you like the boys in their caps?' asked the 'Club Gossip' page, and fans were reminded that trains for the game at Bury on Saturday would be leaving Victoria at 12.30.

First half

Rovers kicked-off towards the Bramall Lane end and passed the ball keenly in the opening minutes. However, with only five minutes gone the home team were in front. The ball was worked down the left-hand side and then across to Bennett who, in space, shot fiercely past Knowles.

Any illusions that the game would be easy for United were almost immediately dispelled, as within a minute of the restart Proudfoot touched the ball to Wilkie, who beat Foulke with a low shot into the corner. Shortly after, Foulke saved well from Campbell, then Killean struck the bar with a fine shot that beat the United 'keeper all ends up. Swinging back and forth, the action continued. Needham had a shot cleared off the line and an excellent header from a United corner by Howell was well saved by Knowles.

After 19 minutes, United were again in front. Needham mishit a shot, but Almond was there to seize on the loose ball and fire home. But again Rovers came back. A free-kick was struck fiercely by Booth, glanced off another player, deflecting past Foulke for the equaliser. A minute later another Rovers shot struck the post but, fortunately for United, deflected wide. Towards half-time both teams did plenty of pressing but no further breakthroughs came.

Second half

The match settled down a little after the break. Early on United gained several corners but were unable to break through a Rovers defence that was now being excellently marshalled by Brandon. Rovers themselves were now proving far less potent in attack and were restricted to a couple of long shots, which were easily dealt with by Foulke. United, taking control, had Almond hit the bar and the same player then put Bennett through to score, but the goal was ruled out for offside.

Eventually United got their noses in front, the goal coming after 75 minutes from the penalty spot. In a goalmouth scramble, Brandon had kept the ball out of the Rovers net by using his hands. At first it seemed as though the referee had missed the incident, but with the crowd howling and both linesmen flagging he then consulted his officials and awarded the kick. As Needham shaped to take it – he'd now taken over the spot-kick duties after Bennett's miss against Preston – he was confronted by the gamesmanship of Knowles, who 'waved his arms as wildly as he could…[and]…proceeded to make something of a human windmill of himself.' Unaffected, Needham coolly slotted it home to put United 3–2 up.

The final quarter of an hour saw United's captain at his imperious best, showing supreme skill and commitment at both ends of the pitch as the game went into a fiercely competitive phase. Needham's emergence coincided with an injury to Rovers' left-half Booth, which left him struggling to cope with Bennett's pace and Needham's forward runs. Bennett beat Killean and sent in a shot that went just wide, while Glover shot just over for the visitors. At this point a weak clearance by Howell was picked up by Needham, who then dribbled through three opponents and added his second with a terrific shot. Not resting on his laurels, 'Nudger' was then to be found at the other end, foiling Wilkie's attempt to score.

With two minutes to go, Bennett, after a good run, forced a corner. From the resultant kick, an almighty scramble ensued in the Blackburn area. Howell shot, Knowles saved, but he could only parry the ball to Morren, whose own shot rebounded off a defender to Needham, who fired home his hat-trick goal. As the whistle blew, the fans were ecstatic, the final three goals giving them the perfect result to round off a superb game of football.

Assessments

The game seemed fairly well balanced until the last quarter of an hour. Certainly some felt the injury to Blackburn's Booth opened up the Rovers' right, but there was no denying Needham's excellent performance in the latter stages. There was a general feeling that United's reorganisation of the front line had been a great success, and the official club reaction reflected this view. The team changes had worked 'fairly well, and all things considered we have no reason to worry about the reserve force for our team.' (Reserves programme, home versus Doncaster, 9 October 1897) Yet a critical eye was cast over all the players. New man Cunningham was 'over anxious' to begin with, but soon 'his passing was smart and good' and he 'will do better yet'. Almond had tried hard, but was not quite there as a centre-forward. 'Perhaps it was asking too much of him to successfully fill in a position in which others had been failures. He worked hard but where he failed was close in.' Whitham was praised for his covering work, but it was acknowledged that his day had gone: he was 'a success though not the back that Thickett is.'

Bennett had again 'played a great game', but the real star had been Needham – 'his shooting was a thing to be remembered…those two last goals were goals to dream about – both rippers.'

Table

		P	W	L	D	Pts
1.	United	7	4	0	3	11
2.	Villa	7	5	2	0	10
3.	Derby	6	3	2	1	7
4.	Sunderland	5	3	1	1	7
5.	Stoke	6	3	2	1	7

United's fixture being on a Monday, it allowed them to leapfrog Aston Villa and go back to the top of the table.

MATCH NO. 8

BURY, AWAY, 9 OCTOBER 1897

Result: Bury 2: *Henderson, Plant*

United 5: *Needham, Bennett, Almond, Morren, Cunningham*

Half-time: 2–2

Attendance: 5,531, Gigg Lane

Teams:

Bury: Montgomery, Darroch, Barbour, Pray, Clegg, Ross, Cust, Garside, Millar, Henderson, Plant.

United: Foulke, Thickett, Cain, Howell, Morren, Needham, Bennett, McKay, Almond, Cunningham, Priest.

Referee: Mr J. Grant (Liverpool)

With Thickett having recovered from injury, he returned to the United side in place of Whitham.

First half

Almond kicked-off for United in fair but dull conditions, and soon the visitors were in control of the game, Bury proving far less determined in the early phase of the play than they had at Bramall Lane. 'The United half-backs were playing grandly and Needham was frequently cheered for his clever play.' (*Independent*) McKay was also 'playing a particularly tricky game…repeatedly outwitting his opponents, giving his partners some capital passes.' After 15 minutes, United's dominance paid off, as Needham beat Montgomery with a shot from the left wing. Surprisingly, the lead was relatively short lived, as five minutes later Bury equalised. A Barbour free-kick was floated into the area, and as Foulke came for it he was charged and unable to collect the ball, which was gratefully knocked into the net by Henderson.

Lifted by their success, the home team now came more into the match. However, unlike United, who were creating some good openings, the Bury strikers lacked penetration in front of goal. Smart work by Almond in midfield led to the centre-forward playing the ball to McKay, who passed it to Bennett. Twisting and turning the 'Shakers' defence, he made himself room to send a vicious low shot past Montgomery. Again, Bury responded to the challenge and had soon equalised. Cust passed the ball through to Plant, Foulke failed to clear and the left-winger made it two-all.

Second half

After six minutes, United again re-established their lead. Priest combined with Cunningham on the left and then sent in a cross, which Montgomery was unable to clear, allowing Almond to nip in to score. With Bury appealing for offside, the referee consulted with both his linesmen and allowed the goal to stand. Bury were again sparked into action. Both sides now created chances as the play flowed from end to end. It was United, however, who struck again. From a tussle in the Bury goalmouth following a corner, the ball was fired towards goal, only for Montgomery to make an excellent block. Unfortunately for the Bury 'keeper the ball fell to Morren, who smashed it into the net past his despairing dive.

It was now United who were dominant and Bennett, McKay and Cunningham all went close. There was then a worrying moment for United as their skipper, Needham, had to be carried from the field having been kicked in the ribs. Fortunately, 'Nudger' was just dazed and winded and was able to return to the field. In his absence, however, came a moment of controversy. Bury stormed down to the United end and there was a huge appeal for a penalty, as Thickett appeared to handle the ball. After consulting both linesmen, however, the referee awarded a free-kick to United – a decision met with howls of derision from the home supporters – ruling that Thickett had been illegally charged from behind. With three minutes to go, United rounded off their performance with a fifth goal. Bennett eluded Barbour out on the right and crossed into the Bury area. The defence scrambled the ball clear, but Howell collected, passed it to Cunningham, who fired the ball past Montgomery.

Assessments

For the second match running, United had hit five goals and clearly there was a growing belief that the changes up front were the answer to earlier problems. The *Telegraph's* headlines were positive: 'Brilliant United Victory'; 'Bury Badly Beaten' and the optimism was shared by the *Independent's* 'centre-forward', who commented on 'an excellent all round display of football' with 'scarcely a weak man in the team'. Not only was their satisfaction with the forwards but 'too much praise cannot be given to the half-backs, who have seldom, if ever, been seen to better advantage.' Bury, who had been a tough nut to crack at Bramall lane and dangerous up front, 'were given fewer opportunities.'

A good assessment of the United performance and their style of play was given by a Bury correspondent in a Lancashire newspaper (quoted in the Preston programme 23 October 1897):

'They simply mopped the floor with us…the forwards don't indulge in draught-board studies in passing. Bang goes the ball from wing to wing, or centre to wing, just where the defence is weakest…like hounds on the trail, they go direct for goal, without any doubling, and when they get there they shoot like demons. Halfbacks and backs are a formidable lot. They are all giants in play, but the halves are a surprising trio of little big "uns".'

Table

		P	W	L	D	Pts
1.	United	8	5	0	3	13
2.	Villa	8	5	2	1	11
3.	Sunderland	6	4	1	1	9
4.	Wednesday	8	4	4	0	8

Other results

West Brom 1–1 Villa
Sunderland 2–1 Derby
Wednesday 3–0 Bolton

MATCH NO. 9

WEDNESDAY, AWAY, 16 OCTOBER 1897

Result: Wednesday 0

United 1: *Bennett*

Half-time: 0–1

Attendance: 24,000, Olive Grove

Teams:

Wednesday: Massey, Earp, Langley, Brandon, Crawshaw, Jamieson, Brash, Ferrier, Kaye, Brady, Spiksley.

United: Foulke, Thickett, Cain, Howell, Morren, Needham, Bennett, McKay, Almond, Cunningham, Priest.

Referee: Mr J.B. Brodie (Wolverhampton)

Rivalry between the officials, players and supporters of both the leading Sheffield clubs had developed very quickly after United's formation in 1889. Derby games, as today, were generating a huge amount of interest within the city. With United top of the League and Wednesday having hit a period of good form, following a disastrous start – they had lost their first three games – the game at Olive Grove was being eagerly anticipated by both sets of supporters. The United football committee were confident that their team would receive lots of support: 'Next Saturday every one of you will be at Olive Grove…display your colours prominently, and do not strike them whether fortune smile or frown.' The pride and loyalty of supporters to both teams was firmly established and to date the bragging honours were very much in the United camp. In the eight games played at Olive Grove since 1893, United had only lost once and won four times. This time, however, Wednesday were expected to prove a tough proposition.

First half

United lost the toss and were forced to defend the goal at the City end with the sun in their eyes and the wind against them.

The action started almost immediately. In the opening minute Almond forced a corner, but the Wednesday defence cleared and it was soon Foulke who was busy, being forced into two smart saves. After just four minutes, United had the lead. Cunningham cut into the centre, laid off the ball to Bennett, who fired home past Massey to the jubilation of the United supporters.

It was all action now, as first United and then Wednesday had goals disallowed. With Almond being carried off after receiving a nasty knee injury, United were down to 10 men and put under a spell of pressure by their opponents. However, United's half-back line were playing superbly. Morren was outstanding at centre-half; Needham's tackling was excellent. Wednesday's danger man, the talented England international left-winger Fred Spiksley, was being closely watched by Howell, who was denying him any room to manoeuvre as soon as he received the ball.

Yet for all Wednesday's pressure, United still remained dangerous, and a superb run through the home defence by Priest ended with him shooting just inches wide of the post. Even more impressive was the work of Bennett who, receiving the ball in midfield, sailed past three opponents before unleashing a powerful shot, which skimmed off the top of the Wednesday bar. It was an effort 'almost electrical in its brilliancy'. (*Telegraph*) Bennett was proving quite a handful for the Wednesday defence, ably assisted by the clever McKay.

Just before half-time, Almond finally returned to the field, but unfortunately was clearly lame. He was unable to make any significant contribution to the action for the rest of the game.

Second half

With Almond already a passenger, United had further bad luck early in the half as the game was stopped for an injury to Bennett. Although the right-winger continued, he too was clearly struggling to keep up with the play. Nevertheless, the game continued to be well contested, though clearly Wednesday had the upper hand. Brady and Spiksley combined well on Wednesday's left, the resultant shot well blocked and then cleared by Cain. Spiksley then contrived to miss a good chance. Perhaps thinking their luck could not get any worse with regard to injuries, United's players and supporters were stunned as Priest was now injured in a collision and his effectiveness, too, was seriously reduced for the rest of the game.

Towards the end Wednesday had the majority of the play, and they forced a succession of corners. However, a combination of solid defending from United and the uncertainty of the Wednesday forwards in front of goal meant that no equaliser could be found. In fact, near the final whistle United could have scored a second. Unfortunately the chance fell to Priest who, being injured, was unable to take advantage. The ball hit the bar, dropped at his feet, only for the left-winger to knock it wide.

Assessments

The game had been a typical derby, full of 'blood and thunder' and commitment from both sides. As is often the case with such games, the magnitude of the occasion will necessarily provide for an exciting game, but one where quality is often lacking. Generally, assessment of the game itself saw the match in this same light, the *Independent's* 'centre-forward' declaring 'The greatness of the occasion proved too much for the eager, anxious contending players, and the quality of the play suffered in consequence.'

Generally, it was felt that a draw had been a fair result, but there was concern that the game had, at times, been too fiercely contested. Almond, Bennett and Priest of United and Crawshaw of Wednesday all ended the game with significant injuries. 'Looker On' in the *Telegraph* singles out Brandon and Howell as particularly over-enthusiastic in their challenges at times. However, such action was not necessarily spiteful but 'due to over-excitement and were the natural outcome of the wild and senseless outbursts from the crowd'.

The conduct of the fans was becoming something of a concern for the press and authorities in Sheffield at the time. In particular, 'derby' matches were gaining a reputation for unruly behaviour, which detracted from the play on the pitch. In an age where professionalism was new in the world of football and the amateur ethic still dominated among the game's authorities, the press and polite society, such fierce partisanship was not to be commended. 'Looker On' strictly censured the crowd's behaviour and the repercussions it had on the players' own performances in the game: 'Scores of really good sportsmen are heartily glad' when such matches are over due to 'the bad blood too often engendered and the unhealthy, almost ferocious, excitement manifested by the crowd. Such a frenzy is essentially unhealthy...there have been matches between Wednesday and United in the past, which have called up worse exhibitions of temper both on the field and in the crowd than was the case on Saturday, but there were plenty of instances even in this most recent game, of conduct which one does not like to see.' (Looker On).

One particular aspect of crowd behaviour that was deplored at the time, although something accepted as the norm today, was the verbal abuse of the referee. Referee, Mr Brodie, had not necessarily had a good game, a lot of stoppages adding to the players' frustrations. Yet the crowd's 'behaviour towards the referee – hooting and howling over decision after decision – was extremely bad.'

However, in terms of the football, United, with three injured players, had definitely impressed, the performance of United's half-backs being of special note – a point also taken up by the club itself: 'it was the display of our halves that cut up the home team. Morren could not have done better; Howell played a rare game, while Ernest Needham was a gem.' (Preston programme, 23 October 1897) Others were also praised: 'Foulke played a big game...the way in which he stopped Spiksley in the first minute was a treat.' – 'It is wonderful how tricky little McKay had got to be. He has a host of funny bits of play which delighted the crowd on Saturday and he is a rare partner for Bennett.' – 'Cunningham too, does well, if he were a shade faster he'd be a capital help.'

Bob Cain was especially praised for his good performance, given that his wife had recently given birth and the baby had kept him awake for half of the preceding week.

On a final note, the ability of United to overcome their injury problems and obtain the victory led 'centre-forward' to declare 'there is now better hope of the League Championship coming to Sheffield than there ever has been before.' Yet there was also a warning. In past seasons United had started well, but this had often been 'followed by a lamentable falling off', so it was felt that the next four fixtures would be crucial – if they were still top then, perhaps United really could do it.

Table

		P	W	L	D	Pts
1.	United	9	6	0	3	15
2.	Aston Villa	9	6	2	1	13
3.	Everton	7	4	2	1	9
4.	Sunderland	7	4	2	1	9

Other results
Villa 4–2 Notts County
Everton 3–0 Liverpool
Sunderland 0–2 West Brom

MATCH NO. 10

PRESTON, HOME, 23 OCTOBER 1897

Result: United 2: *McKay, Needham*
              Preston 1: *Eccleston*

Half-time: 1–0
Attendance: 10,500

Teams:

United: Foulke, Thickett, Cain, Howell, Morren, Johnson, Bennett, McKay, Cunningham, White, Needham.

Preston: Trainer, Holmes, Tait, Hunter, Sanders, Matthews, Eccleston, Stevenson, Brown, Pierce, Boyd.

Referee: Mr Barker (Hanley)

Given the injuries at Olive Grove, United were forced into team changes as only Bennett was sufficiently recovered to play. Almond was replaced by White, making his last appearance for the club, while the versatile Ernest Needham was moved to the left wing to replace Priest. Into Nudger's place came Harry Johnson for his League debut. The switching of Needham was to prove highly successful, and it is interesting to note that the match programme contained a passage from the *Athletic News* that had praised Nudger's performance in the fixture at Preston in early September: 'I know of no cooler player…[he] not only tackles well, but also feeds his forwards, a strong point in a half-back which is often lacking, and shoots well into the bargain.'

Although United had won well in the earlier fixture, in the previous season it had been Preston who had ended their unbeaten run with a 1–0 home victory on 24 October. Given that United's current record was clearly being targeted by their opponents, there was some nervousness around Bramall Lane.

Meanwhile, off the pitch United were opening their new covered stand on Shoreham Street. The admission was priced at 3d. It had been hoped that County Cricket chairman Mr Michael Ellison would open the stand, but as he was unavailable the official opening was cancelled.

First half

Preston lost the toss and kicked-off towards Shoreham Street. For the early stages of the game United were on top, and Trainer was forced into making saves from Needham, Cunningham, McKay, White and Bennett. Preston slowly came into the game themselves, but after half an hour they found themselves a goal down. Needham raced away down the left wing, crossed into the centre, where McKay, racing in, headed the ball past Trainer. Immediately after the restart, United almost had two. Again, Needham charged down the left, sending in a fine, swinging cross which Preston were grateful to put behind the net. From the resulting corner, a shot just went over the Preston bar. With no further scoring, United went in at half-time a goal to the good.

Second half

The game remained comfortable for United, and they were able to go two up thanks to a fine effort from the excellent Needham, revelling in his new forward role. This finally stirred the visitors into action, and as United became rather nervous there was a sustained period of Preston pressure. Finally, after 78 minutes Cain miskicked the ball to Eccleston, who fired past Foulke into the corner of the net. For the rest of the game the play was end to end, yet neither side was able to score again.

Assessments

It had ended up a tight game, yet United had again triumphed and a mark of their progress was seen in the fact that whereas Preston had defeated them twice in the previous season, it was now United who had done the double over their opponents. Johnson was generally seen to have had a successful debut, while Needham had been superb: 'It was in front of goal that United were the better team, thanks chiefly to the grand play of Needham in the unusual position for him on the outside-left.' (Centre-forward – *Independent*)

Table

		P	W	L	D	Pts
1.	United	10	7	0	3	17
2.	Villa	10	6	2	2	14
3.	Everton	8	5	2	1	11
4.	Sunderland	8	4	2	2	10

Other results

Bury 0–1 Everton

Sunderland 0–0 Aston Villa

Match No. 11

Everton, away, 30 October 1897

Result: Everton 1: *Bell*

United 4: *Cunningham, Almond (2), Bennett*

Half-time: 1–3

Attendance: 33,000 Goodison Park, receipts approx £753

Teams:

Everton: McFarlane, Meehan, Storrier, Boyle, Holt, Robertson, Taylor, Divers, Cameron, Williams, Bell.

United: Foulke, Thickett, Cain, Howell, Morren, Needham, Bennett, McKay, Almond, Cunningham, Priest.

Referee: Unknown

There were fears before the game that United would not field a full strength side, 'but careful and judicious training overcame the difficulty and George Waller is to be highly complimented in his success in this direction.' United were back with the team that had faced Wednesday. Needham dropped back to his usual position of left-half, as Fred Priest returned to the left wing and Almond was back as centre-forward. With United still unbeaten there was a growing interest nationally in their continued progress and there was much speculation that Everton, third in the League and with two games in hand, would provide the stiffest test so far. The build up to the game had been quite intense on Merseyside, as Everton's players and supporters were confident that they would end United's run. John Stewart, the Everton captain, destined not to play in the game, had raised the competitive edge by publicly declaring that the 'Toffees' would win, although to be fair he did acknowledge that United 'are a fine side.' The interest on Merseyside was reflected in Sheffield, where both railway companies ran special excursion trains to the game and 1,000 United fans were there to give a vociferous welcome to the team. They, together with the partisan Everton crowd, contributed to a fantastic atmosphere at Goodison Park.

First half

Everton were clearly up for the game and started in determined mood. After only four minutes they had the lead, as Bell smashed the ball past Foulke. For the next few minutes it seemed that United were in danger of being overwhelmed as Everton continued to attack. Holt passed the ball through to Bell, who put the ball in the net, but fortunately this time it was ruled out for offside. United also had Foulke to thank, the 'keeper revelling in the charged atmosphere and making some fine saves to keep his team in the game. After the first quarter of an hour United, having weathered the early pressure, began to get into the game. Cunningham headed wide from a Bennett centre and then Morren hit a shot just over the bar. On 19 minutes United were level. Everton's Meehan hit a careless pass to Storrier, which Cunningham gratefully intercepted and smashed past McFarlane. For the next 10 minutes the game was evenly poised, both sides building dangerous attacks, but on the half-hour mark it was the visitors who broke the deadlock. After Priest had missed out, with only the 'keeper to beat, Cunningham fed Almond, who scored with a fine shot. Everton soon thought they'd levelled the scores as Cameron put the ball in the net from a free-kick, only for it to be disallowed for offside. Spurred on, Everton continued to search for the equaliser and Foulke was forced into another excellent save, this time from Taylor. Shortly after, the same player shot just over the United bar.

Five minutes before half-time the visitors stunned the home crowd and delighted the travelling fans by scoring a third. Almond beat Holt, passed the ball out to Priest, who headed towards the left corner flag and then, beating Meehan, put over an excellent cross which Almond, racing into the centre, headed firmly into the net.

Second half

The game continued in an exciting fashion, even though the play was a little scrappy. Foulke's good form continued as he made a fine clearance from Bell and then made a superb diving save, turning away a Boyle shot which seemed destined for the top corner. Everton were pressing hard to get themselves back into the game, but their forwards lacked the final quality necessary to penetrate United's excellent half-back line, Needham, Morren and Howell doing their usual sterling work. Foulke, too, seemed unbeatable and made another stupendous save as Taylor's excellent cross was met by a thumping Cameron header which seemed to be destined for the net. Yet United were clearly still dangerous. Everton had already been given a warning by Bennett, who had whipped the ball past McFarlane and raced into the box, only for a last gasp intervention by Storrier to force his shot wide. United had appealed strongly for a penalty, claiming Storrier had fouled the winger, but the referee waved them away.

Bennett, however, was not to be denied and, seizing hold of the ball, he proceeded to dribble past Holt, Boyle, Storrier and finally Meehan, before smashing the ball past McFarlane – 'one of the most brilliant individual efforts ever witnessed'. (*Independent*)

Trailing four goals to one, the Everton fans realised their team was beaten and they began to stream away from the ground. To give credit to Everton, the players continued to try, but there was to be no breakthrough. Everton forward Bell, the ex-Wednesday man, clearly seemed to be frustrated with the situation and foolishly got involved in a moment of petulance with United's giant 'keeper Foulke. As the ball was played through he seemed intent on 'capsizing Foulke'. However, the United 'keeper raced out and launched himself towards the ball. Punching it clear, he landed right on top of Bell, who lay prostrate on the ground. Badly winded, though not seriously hurt, Bell had to be carried from the field. The response of the Everton fans was to throw stones at 'Little Willy' – who seemed to be little concerned, although the referee did caution the crowd. Coolly, United's defence closed the game out for a notable victory.

Assessments

It was an excellent victory for United; the high point of their season so far. It had been a keen contest between two very committed teams, and only Bennett's final goal had settled matters. The press believed the key performance had been that of Foulke. 'Simply magnificent. The United custodian had a big say in the decisive victory of his team.' (*Independent*) This was a view echoed by the club: 'Foulke has never kept a better goal than he did on Saturday, and he saved more than once when it looked long odds on his being beaten.' (*Corinthians Programme*, 6 November 1897)

Yet so pleased were all at Bramall Lane with the victory, that credit was given out in all directions: 'Thickett's was something of a roving commission...excellently executed; while Cain was as steady as a rock and never failed.' The half-back line 'all were grand', Morren especially. The forwards were again excellent, 'the whole string worked like a clock.'

United's half-back line were certainly grabbing a lot of attention for their key role in keeping the team at the top of the table. J.J. Bentley, a member of the FA International Selection Committee, had recently commented in the *Sporting Chronicle* 'I like the little trio of half-backs; they are the best I have ever seen,' yet also noted that 'anyone who saw the trio in the street would laugh if they were pointed out as the finest in the kingdom!'

Perhaps remarkable to us, from our distance in time, are the reports of the exuberance of the travelling supporters, as they returned to Sheffield following the victory: '…it was like a final tie to see the enthusiasm on the way home. The trippers shouted, sang, told the porters tales when the train stopped, whistled all the tunes of the universe and, when they reached the Heeley Station, made the "antient welkin" ring afresh by a hullabaloo that might have been heard at Duffum!'

Table

		P	W	L	D	Pts
1.	United	11	8	0	3	19
2.	Villa	11	7	3	2	16
3.	Wolves	10	4	3	3	11
4.	Bolton	9	5	3	1	11
5.	Everton	9	5	3	1	11

Other results

Villa 3–1 Liverpool
Wolves 3–1 Notts Co
Bolton 1–0 Sunderland

MATCH NO. 12

DERBY, AWAY, 13 NOVEMBER 1897

Result: Derby 1: *Maconnochie*
            United 1: *McKay*

Half-time   1–1
Attendance: 10,000, Baseball Ground

Teams:
Derby: Fryer, Methven, Staley, Cox, A. Goodall, Turner, Maconnochie, Bloomer, J. Goodall, Stevenson, McQueen.
United: Foulke, Thickett, Cain, Howell, Morren, Needham, Bennett, McKay, Almond, Cunningham, Priest.

Referee: Mr J.B. Brodie (Wolverhampton)

United continued unchanged after their victory at Everton. The Midland Railway Company put on another special excursion to the game 'and a goodly number of Sheffielders took advantage'. (*Independent*) There had been heavy rain in Derby since Friday afternoon, leaving the pitch treacherous and muddy, conditions similar to when the sides had met on the opening day of the season at Bramall Lane.

First half
Derby's J. Goodall won the toss and forced United to play into a stiff breeze with the rain in their faces.

The Rams were first out of the blocks, Maconnochie feeding Bloomer, who fired his shot into the side netting. United quickly responded, Fryer making an excellent save, tipping the ball over the bar from a fine shot by Needham. Yet it was the home side who were getting on top, and United's defence was hard pressed to keep them at bay. When Cain failed to find distance with a clearance, Maconnochie latched on to the loose ball and fired it past Foulke. Although the

United players appealed strenuously for offside, Mr Brodie waved them away and the goal stood.

With only 16 minutes gone, the sides were level again. United were awarded a free-kick, Howell played in a cross and McKay stole in to head home. In difficult conditions, Derby's forwards had the advantage of the wind and consequently looked more dangerous for the rest of the half. Nevertheless, there were two goalmouth scrambles in the Derby area, their defence relieved to get the ball to safety on each occasion.

Second half

Unfortunately for United, after the interval the rain had stopped and the wind had dropped considerably, therefore depriving the visitors of the advantages enjoyed by their opponents in the first half. Derby's players had used the break to change into clean shirts; United's men carried on regardless.

With the pitch exceedingly heavy, the exertions of the players were beginning to tell and the game's pace slowed. Both defences were generally on top, and when Cunningham did create an opening for Almond to fire home the goal was disallowed for offside. Following this, United were hit with further misfortune when Bennett was carried off, having injured his knee in a collision with Turner. Although he later returned to the pitch, the winger was effectively a passenger for the rest of the game.

In the final quarter of an hour, United were the more creative team and almost grabbed a second goal when, firstly, Needham shot just wide and Fryer made a smart save from a shot by Priest. However, at the end Derby could have won it as Bloomer and J. Goodall combined well and the latter's shot had to be cleared by Foulke.

Assessments

This was another tough game for United, particularly given the poor conditions. Generally, Derby had adapted better than United, who had played more defensively than they had at Goodison Park. Nevertheless, all things considered, it was a sound result, given that only they and Bury had managed to take a point at the Baseball Ground so far this season.

Table

		P	W	L	D	Pts
1.	United	12	8	0	4	20
2.	Villa	13	8	3	2	18
3.	Bolton	12	7	4	1	15
4.	West Brom	12	5	3	4	14

Other results

Villa 3–0 Everton

West Brom 2–1 Liverpool

Bolton 2–1 Stoke

Match No. 13

Blackburn, away, 20 November 1897

Result: Blackburn 1: *Proudfoot*

United 1: *Cunningham*

Half-time: 1–0

Attendance: 7,000, Ewood Park

Teams:

Blackburn: Knowles, Brandon, Glover, Ball, Booth, Killean, Briercliffe, Hulse, Proudfoot, Wilkie, Campbell.

United: Foulke, Thickett, Cain, Howell, Morren, Needham, Jenkinson, McKay, Almond, Cunningham, Priest.

Referee: Mr A. Green (West Bromwich)

With Bennett's injury at Derby not having cleared up, Thomas Jenkinson came in for his League debut, but otherwise United were unchanged. The Blackburn public were hopeful that they could inflict the first defeat of the season on United, their confidence quite high given that they had defeated Aston Villa at Ewood Park earlier in the season.

The Match

Rovers won the toss and United kicked-off towards the town goal. The first half was competitive, yet Rovers had the better of the earlier exchanges. Young Jenkinson occasionally beat left-back Killean, but generally the absence of Bennett meant that most danger came from the United left. United's three inside-forwards – McKay, Almond and Cunningham – were working hard, but fine defensive work by Rovers kept them at bay.

The home side gradually gained the upper hand and Foulke was forced into a good save from a shot by Campbell. Rovers did go ahead, however, when, from a cross, the ball deflected off a United defender for Proudfoot to head in by the post. Although United appealed for offside, the goal was given.

Just before half-time the injury 'hoodoo' struck United yet again. Almond, going for a ball, slipped, and an opponent landed on top of him. The result was that Almond wrenched his knee and was forced from the pitch for the rest of the half.

Second half

The visitors were back to full strength as Almond returned to the pitch. However, the United man was not very mobile and contributed little of any significance for the rest of the game. United were determined to preserve their unbeaten run and were soon on the attack, Jenkinson passing to McKay whose shot was well saved by Knowles. Needham and the United half-backs were feeding their forwards with some fine passes, and only sterling work by the Rovers backs Brandon and Glover was keeping them at bay. As the game entered the last quarter, the Rovers fans were becoming edgy and nervous, and after Briercliffe, on a rare Rovers break, fired wide it was all United.

With five minutes left the equaliser came. After a period of intense pressure, Cunningham seized on a half-saved shot by Knowles and barged in the rebound. Going all out for victory, the visitors almost scored twice in the last frantic minutes as shots cannoned off Blackburn defenders, with their 'keeper well beaten.

Assessments

United had again come back strongly after going a goal down and had gained a satisfactory point. It was again pleasing how the team had responded to the fact that an injury to a key player, this time Almond, had disadvantaged them. The players were confident and the unbeaten run had continued.

Table

		P	W	L	D	Pts
1.	United	13	8	0	5	21
2.	Villa	14	8	4	2	18
3.	Bolton	13	8	4	1	17
4.	West Brom	13	6	3	4	16

Other results

Bolton 2–0 Aston Villa
West Brom 3–1 Derby

Match No. 14

Nottingham Forest, home, 4 December 1897

Result: United 1: *Almond*

            Forest 1: *McPherson (pen)*

Half-time: 0–0

Attendance: 9,700

Teams:

United: Foulke, Thickett, Cain, Howell, Morren, Johnson, Needham, McKay, Almond, Cunningham, Priest.

Forest: Allsop, Ironmonger, Ritchie, Wragg, McPherson, Frank Forman, McInnis, Arthur Capes, Benbow, Richards, Fred Forman.

Referee: Mr J. Lewis (Blackburn)

Almond had recovered from his knock at Blackburn, but Bennett was still injured. United went for a different option to cover his absence. This time Ernest Needham was shifted to the right wing – he had previously deputised on the left wing for Priest against Preston – and Harry Johnson came in again to take the captain's usual role at left-half.

The match programme noted how, nationally, there was a growing feeling that United's unbeaten run would be bound to come to an end soon. Yet the team had played three tough away games in the League, their last home fixture had been against Preston on 23 October, and it had not happened yet.

Additionally, through the programme, the club produced interim reports on the form and progress of their key players, and their comments prove interesting reading:

Ernest Needham, referring to United's visit to the capital to play a friendly against the leading amateur team Corinthians: 'last Saturday the Londoners nearly went wild over him, and they don't often do that over a northerner'.

Harry Thickett: 'Thickett's rushes are the essences of good judgement and dash. He gets there every time and clears splendidly.'

Rab Howell: '…does all well but shoot. He can't do that.'

Walter Bennett: 'Bennett is still the best outside-right in England, let the Villa say what they like of Athersmith. Nor has he Athersmith's dirtiness. Clearly football goes a long way when a selection committee is on hand; so we vote for Walter.' (The comments on Athersmith can be regarded either as refreshingly honest or merely biased. Such comments on an opposition player would certainly not be seen in an official match programme today.)

Fred Priest: 'Keeps up his request for work. Never tires; always on the ball; and keeps a goalkeeper's eyes open when he shoots. Knows what bull's eye means.'

John Cunningham: 'Cunningham improves every match. He used not to be good enough for Preston reserves. He is good enough for our first.'

Kenny McKay: 'McKay is still as tricky as ever. Makes Bennett a rare partner.'

First half

United started the game very well and for the opening 20 minutes were pressing hard on the Forest defence. The best opportunity to open the scoring came when United were awarded an indirect free-kick three or four yards from their opponents' goalline. As the kick was taken, 'there was a terrific scrimmage somewhat after the rugby order of things' (*Independent*), before Forest managed to scramble the ball away. Priest then fired a great chance over the bar, as did Needham, and Allsop made a couple of fine saves, the best from a fierce shot by Priest.

With the crowd fired up, Forest remained calm, and into the second period of the half they finally began to mount attacks of their own. A good shot from Frank Forman was saved with some difficulty by Foulke, but it was United who were pressing as the half ended. A long-range effort from Cain was only just kept out by Allsop.

Second half

The second half was much more evenly balanced, as Forest came out with a far more attacking performance. Initially, though, United again looked more dangerous and Needham soon grazed the top of the Forest bar with a rasping shot. On 62 minutes 'Nudger' ran down the right, beat two defenders and crossed in. Cunningham, racing in, shot towards goal, Allsop parried and Almond nipped in to score 'amidst enthusiastic cheers'. (*Independent*) The animated crowd were now really behind United, who pressed anew. Yet the Forest defence did not disintegrate and soon their forwards were trying hard to get their team back into the game. A Forest break resulted in a 'scorcher' of a shot from Richards; United grateful for an equally good save from Foulke. Shortly after, Forest forced a couple of corners and the match was now fiercely contested and evenly balanced.

On 73 minutes Forest were level. Thickett appeared to trip McInnis in the United area, and Mr Lewis 'manfully' awarded a penalty 'in spite of the howls of the crowd' (*Independent*), who were furious at the decision. Calmly, McPherson despatched the penalty.

A frenetic last period saw both teams with chances to win. Benbow had a superb opening, following a cross by McInnis, but put the ball over the bar. The last few minutes were all United, but as they had done for most of the game, the Forest defence remained resolute.

Assessments

This was yet another tough game for United, who were finding their opponents determined to do their utmost against the unbeaten League leaders. Forest had defended with guts and resolution and, it could be argued, had earned the necessary good fortune of the penalty decision, which had enabled them to take a point. United had now not won since their great victory at Everton, and, although two of the three games had been away and the team had played well, a hint of frustration was beginning to emerge among some sections of the supporters.

Table

		P	W	L	D	Pts
1.	United	14	8	0	6	22
2.	Villa	15	9	4	2	20
3.	Wolves	15	7	5	3	17
4.	Bolton	14	8	5	1	17

Other results

Wolves 2–0 Derby

MATCH NO. 15

STOKE, AWAY, 11 DECEMBER 1897

Result: Stoke 2: *Hingerty, Hill*

United 1: *Needham*

Half-time: 1–0

Attendance: 6,000, The Victoria Ground

Teams:

Stoke: Johnston, A. Rowley, Eccles, Murphy, Wood, Durber, Pugh, Mellor, Hingerty, Hill, Schofield.

United Foulke, Thickett, Cain, Howell, Morren, Needham, Jenkinson, McKay, Almond, Cunningham, Priest.

Referee: Mr L.W. Furniss

Bennett was still injured, and United gave another outing to Jenkinson, this time leaving Needham in his usual left-half position. It was hoped that United would get back to winning ways, given the relative weakness of their opponents. Reviewing the game, 'centre-forward' was especially confident: 'the League leaders, Sheffield United, will be at Stoke, opposing one of the weakest teams in the competition, and unless something unexpected happens will add two more points to their record.' Stoke's form had certainly been indifferent at home, and they were struggling at the foot of the table. Yet, on the day, heavy downpours had badly affected the pitch. It was treacherous underfoot, with heavy mud and large pools of water covering many areas. The conditions had kept the crowd down to 6,000, it having been expected many more would have attended in the hope that the Potters would be the first team to end United's run.

First half

The game started surprisingly fast, given the state of the pitch. Both sides were eager to attack and play swung from end to end. Early on, the best opportunity came to the visitors, when Cunningham headed against the bar with Johnston well beaten. Yet United's adventurous play proved their undoing on 23 minutes. Bob Cain charged up the field, but when the ball was intercepted by Stoke there was a huge gap on the left of United's defence, as no one had dropped back to cover him. Hingerty moved into the space, received the ball and, advancing, shot easily past Foulke to put the Potters a goal up.

United stormed back but again suffered misfortune with the woodwork. Stoke 'keeper Johnston pushed a free-kick onto the post, which rebounded out for the defence to clear it away. A good passing move – involving Jenkinson, McKay, Almond and Cunningham – made a good opening for Priest, but unfortunately the left-winger shot wide.

Interestingly, the two teams were employing different tactics. United were using a short passing game – instead of their trademark long sweeping passes – to adapt to the muddy conditions. Stoke, meanwhile, were launching the ball long to their wings – the right side of Pugh and Mellor proving particularly troublesome to the United defence. As half-time arrived, neither side could secure another breakthrough.

Second half

Stoke almost doubled their lead straight away as a fine shot by Schofield was turned away for a corner by Foulke. United quickly responded though, and Cunningham only just missed as he hooked a chance just over the Stoke bar. The game was end to end. Stoke had two good chances, Foulke saving well from Hill and Schofield shooting wide. McKay thought he'd equalised for United as he shot home, only to find his goal disallowed for offside.

Stoke were clearly playing above themselves, far better than their League position warranted. United were unable to equalise, and 10 minutes from full time disaster struck as the home side went two up. It was a strange goal and a result of the muddy conditions. Attempting to clear the ball, Thickett slipped. As Hill rushed in to collect, Foulke jumped out to block his shot. Unfortunately, Foulke also lost his footing, and as he lay prostrate on the floor Hill slotted the ball into the empty net.

To their credit, United did not give up and hauled themselves back into the game when Needham and Morren combined and the United captain fired past Johnston. United now continued to press hard, but the equaliser would not come and the game ended with their first League defeat of the season.

Assessments

The result was a surprise to the football world, given the relative positions of the teams. United could claim to be unlucky as they had hit the woodwork twice and had a goal disallowed, and as a result the local press were not too hard on them.

The club themselves were rather put out that many Wednesday supporters had shown a sense of satisfaction that United had been beaten. Their irritation was displayed in the leading comments made in the Bolton programme, in a game destined to be called off, the following Saturday: 'Surely the City first!'; 'Let club prejudice sink until the clubs meet.' It was generally believed that Sheffield locals should be supportive of both clubs, unless playing one another, as both were representatives of the city.

Beyond Sheffield, the national papers had been questioning United's title pedigree for the last couple of weeks. Both the *Sportsman* and *Athletic News* emphasised the fact that United had not won since beating Everton back in October. Clearly their form was on the wane, and was not as fine as it had been. *The Athletic Record* was far more critical, its comment almost reflecting a sense of satisfaction at United's misfortune: 'Sheffield United came a most inglorious cropper at Stoke…it looks as though the United were on the wane and their match with their fellow townsmen – Wednesday – will be eagerly looked for.'

Both *The Umpire* and *Sports* indicated the pleasure there was in Birmingham at United's defeat, Aston Villa supporters now feeling that they themselves would now close in on another Championship.

However, United were not about to throw in the towel, the club declaring with some determination 'the same energy which has carried us to the top will keep us there; and don't you forget it.' (Bolton Programme 18 December 1897)

Table

		P	W	L	D	Pts
1.	United	15	8	1	6	22
2.	Villa	16	10	4	2	22
3.	Wolves	16	8	5	3	19
4.	Wednesday	15	8	5	2	18
5.	West Brom	15	7	4	4	18

Other results

Villa 5–1 Blackburn

Wolves 2–1 Liverpool

Wednesday 2–1 Preston

Forest 0–1 West Brom

Note

When United's match at home to Bolton was abandoned before kick-off on 18 December due to fog, thousands were already inside Bramall Lane. Supporters were given tickets to admit them to any game other than the upcoming Wednesday fixture. Aston Villa's 0–0 draw at Stoke put them a point clear at the top. Playing on Christmas Day, Villa lost 2–1 at Everton so that, before United met Wednesday on 27 December, the relative positions of the top two clubs were:

		P	W	L	D	Pts
1.	Aston Villa	18	10	5	3	23
2.	United	15	8	1	6	22

MATCH NO. 16

WEDNESDAY, HOME, 27 DECEMBER 1897

Result: United 1: *Earp (og)*

Wednesday 1: *Spiksley*

Half-time: 1–0

Attendance: 37,389

Teams:

United: Foulke, Thickett, Cain, Howell, Morren, Needham, Bennett, McKay, Almond, Cunningham, Priest.

Wednesday: Massey, Earp, Langley, Brandon, Crawshaw, Jamieson, Brash, Ferrier, Kaye, Brady, Spiksley.

Referee: Mr Scragg (Crewe)

United were now back to full strength with the return of Bennett. Wednesday, who had won 4–0 against Stoke on Christmas Day (and with United not having played), were now just two points behind their rivals. Wednesday's form had been excellent since their poor start, and they and United had the two best defensive records in the League. The visitors, therefore, had realistic ambitions of aiming for the title themselves, and as a result there was massive interest in the city for days before the fixture. With both sides at full strength, the gates at Bramall Lane were opened at 12.45 and a crowd of over 37,000 had soon packed in, many taking up a vantage point out in the pavilion.

First half

Wednesday emerged onto the pitch first, to a rousing ovation from their fans. United, following them, received equally enthusiastic cheers from their own supporters. Kicking-off, Wednesday had the advantage of playing downwind, but with the rain settling in the pitch was soon very greasy.

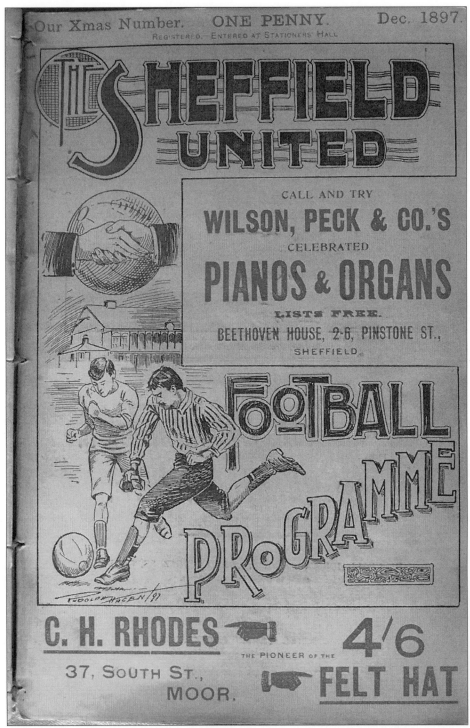

The Christmas issue of *The Sheffield United Programme* from the game versus Sheffield Wednesday, which was specially printed in three colours: red, black and green.

Attacking strongly, Wednesday almost had the lead in the first minute, as a shot by Brady almost beat Foulke. United responded with a long shot from Thickett which Wednesday 'keeper Massey, receiving close attention from Priest, almost fumbled into his own net. But in general it was Wednesday who were creating more problems, and their left-winger Spiksley was proving a particularly tricky customer. When the Wednesday man went down, following a challenge from Thickett, there were huge appeals for a penalty. Fortunately for United, the referee would have none of it. Wednesday continued to press and a couple of fierce shots by Langley, assisted by the wind, were cleared away by Needham and Thickett.

However, United were gradually getting into the game themselves, and the returning Bennett was making some probing runs down the right, as well as forcing Massey into an excellent save from a fierce shot. It was a shot from Bennett on 25 minutes that caused all kinds of problems for the Wednesday 'keeper. The 'keeper was unable to collect it, the ball ran free, and as Earp came to his aid the right-back's attempted clearance sliced into the net, giving United the lead.

Stung by their misfortune, Wednesday went into the attack with renewed vigour, and the home defence were again hard pressed to hold out. Just before half-time, Wednesday thought they had the equaliser. Unfortunately, their direct free-kick had sped directly into the net without touching any other player. As a result, the referee had no option but to disallow the goal.

Second half

The game continued in an attacking vein as both teams sought further goals. Brady and Spiksley were behind most of Wednesday's good work, and when the former played in a cross from the left Brash had only Foulke to beat, but he shot wide. Responding, Almond sent in a fine dipping shot which, although it had Massey beaten, went just over the bar.

The dangerous Spiksley was now being double-marked by Howell and Thickett. The close attention of Howell seemed particularly irksome for the Wednesday man. Yet, finally getting away from them, Spiksley played in a great ball to Kaye. Wednesday's centre-forward should have scored, but Cain managed to block his effort. Unfortunately for the United man, the ball ran back to Spiksley, who smashed it past Foulke for the equaliser.

The game was certainly competitive and the action superb. 'The excitement was intense and the patrons of either team yelled lustily.' (*Telegraph*, 28 December 1897) Again Brash had a 'one on one' with Foulke, but the giant 'keeper came out on top and, regardless of the wave of attacks on both sides, the game ended up with honours even.

ALEXANDRA THEATRE.

Lessees   ...   **THE SHEFFIELD ALEXANDRA THEATRE Co. Ltd.**

Managing Director   ...   .   **Mr. WILLIAM D. FORSDIKE.**

CHRISTMAS HOLIDAYS and **FAIR WEEK**, gigantic production of the GRAND ANNUAL PANTOMIME,

CHRISTMAS EVE, Friday, Dec. 24th, 1897, and every Evening at 8:

DICK ⟶
WHITTINGTON.

Most Powerful Company of Artistes in Sheffield !

Gorgeous Costumes !

Splendid New Scenery !

DAY PERFORMANCES.—Monday, Dec. 27th ; Tuesday, Dec. 28th ; Thursday, Dec. 30th ; Friday, Dec. 31st ; New Year's Day, January 1st, 1898 ; and every Saturday at 2. Early doors open at 1 o'clock.

SPECIAL NOTICE.—The Matinees will be equal in every respect to the Evening Performance.

Doors open at 6.30 ; Performance to commence at 7 o'clock. Centre Boxes 2/6 (Reserved, 3/- ; Side Boxes, 1/- ; Pit, 6d. ; Gallery; 4d. ; Private Boxes, 21/-, to hold four. Box Office open daily from 11 till 3, and throughout evening performances. Early Doors open at 6. Sixpence extra to all parts ; except Gallery, Twopence. No money returned. Seats not guaranteed unless booked.

Half-price at 9 o'clock to Dress Circle and Side Boxes.

THE CITY PANTOMIMES.

"Dick Whittington" at THE ALEXANDRA.

ALWAYS has "t' Alec" held its own in pantomime, and now that the days of the Brittlebanks are gone, the limited company now having charge of the big house by the Sheaf, with Mr. Forsdike an admirable chief, still keeps up its reputation.

For the present year the pantomime is to be on the old familiar lines of *Dick Whittington*.

The scenery is of the type which is associated with this house, done excellently by Mr. Maughan, and it includes the interior of a Cyclops rolling mill, Fitzwarren's shop, Highgate Hill, the docks (not at Sheffield), and so to Morocco and back again. All round, the scenery is of an admirable character, whilst the closing scene of all is a representation of the Alexandra itself.

There are many local allusions in the book, and Mr. Booth has catered specially for Sheffield. Mr. Parkin has composed very tuneful music. Madame Riviere has arranged the ballets and processions, and they are as successful as any of her previous work at the Alexandra. The dresses, produced under the management of Miss Shiells, are charming combinations of rich colours; and advantage has been taken of the electric light installation at the theatre, hundreds of lamps being fixed.

Turning here to the cast, Mr. J. W. Rowley's breezy Yorkshire comedy in the part of the apprentice, Idle Jack, is a great draw. Sprightly Dick is impersonated by that clever artiste, Miss Ella Deane, whose last appearance in pantomime in Sheffield was five years ago; and Miss Jessie Albini, who is not unknown in Sheffield, makes a charming Alice Fitzwarren. The sisters, along with the Brothers Lorenzi—"Bill" and "Bob," the knockabout parts— are noted for their sketches; and a good comedian is the Cook, Mr. Malcolm D. Scott, formerly with *The Water Babes*. Miss Felstead, who took a prominent part in the *Lady Slavey* and Miss Dollie Doyle, who was a pleasing dancer in last year's pantomime, and was in Sheffield a few days ago with *Morocco Bound*, are also included in the cast, taking the Fairy Queen and the Maid to the Princess respectively.

Of course there has to be a capital cat, and that important party in the play will find a capital exponent in Mr. Freddie Farren, who has gained a name for animal impersonation, and was formerly associated with the clever Charles Lauri.

Indeed, the whole cast is a good one, and here, as at the Lyceum, the only thing to say is, "Go and get your seat. You can't go there too soon—after the doors are open."

Christmas won't be Christmas till you've seen this splendid show.

See the preceding page for particulars.

Not everything inside *The Sheffield United Programme* was related to football; here is an advert and review for the Christmas pantomime.

Assessment

The game had been excellent. Most pleasing to the local press was the fact that, unlike the game earlier in the season, it had been a fairly fought contest with few fouls apart from those of an accidental nature. The standard of play exhibited by both sides had been first rate, and so noteworthy had been the occasion that the *Independent* saw fit to pay the following tribute to the teams in its editorial column on the day after the game:

'Yesterday there was little scrambling and less roughness. Both sides played not only their hardest, but their best, and the lover of good football, who usually attends such matches but with little hope of pleasure, thoroughly enjoyed himself. Wednesday showed that they understood the kind of football required for the occasion by their indulgence in long kicking and passing; while United, by their beautifully combined work forward and dogged steadiness at the back, proved that they had returned to their best form, and that the pessimists who considered that the prospect of the championship coming to Sheffield vanished a fortnight ago at Stoke, are dismally premature.'

The club's assessment of the performance (from the programme versus Liverpool on 29 December 1897) was generally positive, but with some points of reservation. 'Needham's grand generalship stood out' – 'our halves were the feature! All three played masterly football.' Yet 'Forward there wasn't the same excellence.' Bennett had taken a knock in the second half and so was not very effective and 'Almond…is not himself; he wants more dash.'

The crowd of 37,389 was a record against Wednesday, and it seemed that United had overcome their stumble against Stoke City.

Table

		P	W	L	D	Pts
1.	Villa	19	10	5	4	24
2.	United	16	8	1	7	23
3.	West Brom	17	8	4	5	21
4.	Wednesday	18	9	6	3	21
5.	Wolves	18	8	5	5	21

Other results

West Brom 1–1 Blackburn

Wolves 1–1 Villa

MATCH NO. 17

LIVERPOOL, HOME, 29 DECEMBER 1897

Result: United 1: *unknown*

Liverpool 2: *McCowie, Thickett (og)*

Half-time: 1–1
Attendance: 4,000

Teams:
United: Foulke, Thickett, Cain, Howell, Johnson, Needham, Bennett, McKay, Almond, Cunningham, Priest.
Liverpool: Storer, Goldie, Dunlop, McCartney, McQue, Cleghorn, Geary, Walker, Hartley, McCowie, Lumsden.

Referee: Mr T. Holme (Farnworth)

United made one change to their line up. With Morren injured, Johnson moved into his place at centre-half. After six games, neither of the sides had beaten the other in the League and another stiff contest was anticipated. Conditions for the game were terrible: a soaking drizzle interspersed with heavy showers and strong gusts of wind. It had actually been raining for several hours, which had resulted in the pitch becoming very heavy and muddy. With the inclement weather and the fact that the game was being played on a Wednesday, the crowd was only 4,000 – a 10th of the bank holiday gate against Wednesday. It seems as though the referee was not eager to take charge of the proceedings, given the conditions. The Liverpool players were on the pitch at 2.15 ready to start, and Mr Holme did not arrive until 2.30. After a two-minute kick about, the visitors promptly went back to the changing rooms and out of the rain.

First half
Needham won the toss and opted to kick towards the Shoreham Street end, with the wind and rain at United's backs. The conditions immediately proved difficult, with

95

passes being held up in the mud and the players slipping and falling on the treacherous surface. It was the Liverpool forwards who adapted more quickly to the conditions, and a good move by them ended with Foulke making a fine diving save from a fierce shot by McCartney. United did hit back. A free-kick from Bennett struck the Liverpool post and rebounded to Priest, whose shot was saved by Storer. After this there followed a spell of pressure by the home side, and, after gaining a corner on 30 minutes, a chaotic goalmouth scramble ensued in the Liverpool area and the ball ended up in the net, with no one sure who had the final touch.

United had the lead but were soon pegged back. Inside two minutes a Liverpool break downfield ended with McCowie beating Foulke with a magnificent shot. Although United pressed hard for the rest of the half, the visitors' defence was thoroughly organised and the home forwards could find no way through. Ominously, Liverpool were defending in depth but always prepared to hit United on the break. On the occasions they did, they looked extremely dangerous.

Second half

United came out in a fresh clean kit, now having to play into the rain and wind that they had been unable to capitalise on in the first half. There was a good early chance for Priest, but he put the ball past the post, unfortunate as United fell behind 10 minutes into the half. Geary sent in a cross from the right, and Thickett, trying to clear, succeeded only in putting the ball through his own net. A minute later it was almost 3–1: 'Hartley sending in a hot shot at close quarters which Foulke saved in marvellous fashion, conceding a corner in the effort.' (*Telegraph*, 30 December 1897) Again Foulke came to the rescue, saving a shot by Walker 'in capital style', and it was clear that the visitors were making far better use of the conditions than United had in the first half.

Finally, United managed to launch some counter-attacks of their own. Priest broke away down the left and moved the ball across to Bennett, who shot just wide. Bennett then sent in a long-range effort that Storer just managed to tip over the bar. As the game entered its final stages, United applied mounting pressure but were unable to create many clear chances against a determined Liverpool defence. Perhaps the best chance of all fell to Almond, but he was unable to convert and the visitors themselves provided Foulke with plenty of action at the other end. Unable to get an equaliser, United suffered their first home defeat of the season.

Assessment

It had been a tough game in difficult conditions, and Liverpool had to be commended on their win. They had adapted better than United, and the speed and passing of their two wingers, Geary and Lumsden, had been excellent. For all that though, there was disappointment with United's defeat. 'Looker-On' in the *Telegraph* noted how United had not performed well in previous games, Derby at home and Stoke away, where the conditions had been wet and muddy. Furthermore, given that United had now gone six League games without a victory, the old criticisms of the forward line, seen earlier in the season, were beginning to resurface. 'Looker-On' noted that 'it was in the forwards where the weakness lay – and unless a new centre-forward is quickly found, or Almond recovers his lost form, we shall have further reverses to chronicle instead of those victories which we had all hoped would carry the team on to the championship. Almond has done nothing ever since the Everton match, and that is a long time ago, while until the last few minutes of yesterday's game Bennett was of no use.'

Journalists were clearly no more sensitive to the sensibilities of the players than their counterparts are today. With such criticism, the players were going to need a strong streak of mental toughness if their title ambitions were to remain intact.

Table

		P	W	L	D	Pts
1.	Villa	19	10	5	4	24
2.	United	17	8	2	7	23
3.	West Brom	18	8	4	6	22
4.	Wolves	19	8	5	6	22

No other games today.

Match No. 18

Notts County, away, 1 January 1898

Result: Notts County 1: *Stewart (pen)*
United 3: *Gaudie (2); Bennett*

Half-time: 1–1
Attendance: 11,000, Trent Bridge

Teams:

Notts County: Toone, Prescott, Lewis, Crone, Calderhead, Stewart, Langham, Carter, Bull, Boucher, Deighton.
United: Foulke, Thickett, Cain, Johnson, Morren, Needham, Bennett, French, Gaudie, Cunningham, Priest.

Referee: Mr West (Lincoln)

Three changes were made to the United line up. Johnson deputised for Howell, at right-half; French made his League debut, replacing fellow Scotsman McKay at inside-right, and Ralph Gaudie came in at centre-forward in place of Almond, also making his League debut. As it was a public holiday, a large following of around 2,000 United supporters journeyed to the game. The fans were to provide excellent vocal backing for the team throughout the match. Although the weather was initially fine and clear, by the end the mist had descended and supporters found much of the action difficult to follow.

First half

United won the toss and decided to defend the Gamston Lane end. County attacked right from the start and almost immediately Deighton fired the ball past Foulke. However, the referee disallowed the goal for offside. It was now United's turn, and with just two minutes gone Bennett beat Lewis out on the right and crossed the ball into the centre. Gaudie controlled the cross and then coolly slotted home – Toone getting a hand to the ball but unable to keep it out.

It was a frenetic start to the game, and the pace was not about to slacken. County again had the ball in United's net, this time from Langham, but again it was disallowed for offside. On 10 minutes, the equaliser finally arrived. Bull was tripped in the area by Thickett and Stewart put away the resulting penalty.

The play continued from end to end. For United, Bennett was making some excellent runs down the right and Gaudie, clearly enjoying his opportunity in the side, put in another good shot. For County, right-winger Langham was proving a real handful, and Foulke was forced into a fine short-range stop from Bull. As the end of the half approached, it was United who were beginning to get on top. Needham and Gaudie combined to move the ball downfield, the former ending the move with a fierce shot that just grazed the top of the bar. Following this, both Priest and Morren had efforts that went close. Nevertheless, a couple of attacks by the home side, as the half ended, reminded United that they still had a contest on their hands

Second half

It took United some time to re-emerge for the second period, but the team were soon into their stride with Cunningham sending in a good shot that was saved by Toone. County then stormed back and Foulke was forced into two excellent saves. The home side was now getting on top and their vociferous supporters were creating a hostile environment, all the more important then that the travelling fans were giving the United men as much encouragement as they could. Having denied their team two goals in the first half, the home support was particularly venomous towards Mr West, the referee. The *Telegraph* noted how their behaviour was 'In very bad form and time after time [they] hooted the referee without the least cause, while the language of those in front of the press box was abominable.' Yet for all the County pressure the United goal remained intact, largely due to the excellent form of their goalkeeper 'Foulke being unbeatable, though again and again he was called upon with big work to do, doing it all in rare fashion.'

Somewhat against the run of play, United took the lead in the 65th minute. From a United shot the ball cannoned off a County defender and out to Bennett on the right who, with a fine, low shot, crashed the ball across the area and into the far corner of the net. After this the home crowd started to vent their frustration, particularly around the poor Sheffield journalists in the press box, and this began to affect the play on the pitch: 'the game was by no means a pleasant one, and the temper of the crowd imparted itself to the players, with the result that collisions and those not of the lightest, were frequent.'

The action and attacking play now continued unabated from both sides. A Needham shot was cleared by Prescott off the line, the ball ricocheting to Deighton, who ran half the length of the field to fire in a shot that was magnificently put around the post by Foulke.

The mist was now lying thickly across the pitch as the game entered the last 10 minutes. United were being heavily pressed: 'Fouls were indulged in indiscriminately by the Notts men as the visitors increased the pressure and the referee had a very difficult task on hand.' With five minutes to go, United finally made the game safe. Priest turned Crone inside-out on the left and crossed into Gaudie who, with a smart, low shot, scored United's third. With their team beaten, the County fans now streamed towards the exits, leaving the United supporters jubilant. Well on top for the last few minutes, United had their first League win since 30 October.

Assessment

It had been another very tough game for United. County had been physically strong and had played to a far better standard than their position at the foot of the table warranted. It was an even contest, but Gaudie had proved an effective replacement at centre-forward, scoring twice on his League debut, and the form of United's 'keeper had been superb. The club were delighted with their custodian, and declared 'Foulke was at his best. He thumped out the big ones, punched those he could not fist, scooped away those along the ground, and flung himself bodily at others…' (Aston Villa Home programme, 8 January 1898)

Important to the victory had been the 2,000 travelling fans, and the club noted 'Our trippers were delighted with the victory, and we had quite a reception when we reached Sheffield station.'

It was a crucial win for United. It had ended their barren spell without a victory and put them back to the top of the table – an excellent morale booster given that their next two fixtures were against their leading title rivals Aston Villa.

Table

		P	W	L	D	Pts
1.	United	18	9	2	7	25
2.	Villa	19	10	5	4	24
3.	West Brom	19	8	4	7	23
4.	Wolves	19	8	5	6	22

Other results

Liverpool 1–1 West Brom

MATCH NO. 19

ASTON VILLA, HOME, 8 JANUARY 1898

Result: United 1: *Bennett*
               Aston Villa 0

Half-time: 1–0
Attendance: 23,887

Teams:

United: Foulke, Thickett, Cain, Howell, Morren, Needham, Bennett, McKay, Gaudie, Cunningham, Priest.

Aston Villa: Whitehouse, Bowman, Evans, B. Sharpe, James Cowan, Crabtree, Athersmith, Harvey, Devey, Wheldon, John Cowan.

Referee: Mr J. Lewis (Blackburn) – rated as one of the strongest in England

Both teams fielded very strong line ups. Gaudie continued at centre-forward for United, the amateur from South Bank given preference over Almond following his two goals at Notts County, while Villa preferred Whitehouse to George in goal. George was Villa's usual number one but had been suspended; he was now available for selection, but given he would not be able to play in future Cup ties Villa decided to stick with Whitehouse. Devey and Athersmith had both just returned from injury. Although Villa were pressing United hard in the title race, their form was short of that shown in the previous season when they had won the title with an impressive 47 points. Consistency seemed to be lacking, and the *Sports Argus* in Birmingham had declared 'their warmest admirers will scarcely claim that they are now playing anything approaching the game…in the second half of the last season…though public confidence in Sheffield United has been shaken by their late performances…there will be a good deal of surprise if the Villans pull off the Championship again.' (1 January 1898) Nevertheless, there was a massive national interest in the game and many spectators were brought in from other areas by special excursion trains. Locally, there was of course huge anticipation and excitement among the United following. The *Telegraph's* 'Looker On', in his preview of the fixture, just hoped that the standard of play would match the importance of the occasion: 'too often in these games players, by their own excitement, fail to produce their best form, but it is to be hoped that…the games will be brimful of that fine football which both teams are capable of.' ('Looker On', *Telegraph*, 8 January 1898)

The United football committee was certainly determined to win the game and bring the title to Sheffield, showing their commitment by funding special residential training measures for the team at the Chesterfield Hydro at Matlock Bank, during the week prior to the game. It was a controversial move, as for the whole week no ball work was done by the players. The theory was that when the game came around, the United team would be desperate to get hold of the ball – 'as eager for it as a cat for a mouse.' ('Looker On', *Telegraph*, 8 January 1898) The focus of the sessions was on fitness, it being reported that 'the whole team, however it is constituted, may be depended upon to toe the mark in tip top form, and give the Villa a rare battle.' When the United committee had announced the special training measures to the press on Tuesday, the Villa committee became so concerned that they immediately sent their own team to Droitwich for special brine baths – determined to ensure the United men should get no advantage in their preparations for the match. All of this added, of course, to the great interest surrounding the game.

On Saturday morning the team left Matlock by train at 10.56, arriving at Midland Station at 12.23. The excitement of United's fans was shown by the fact that a large crowd had assembled to meet them and then cheered them loudly as they were driven to the Lane.

The fine weather in Sheffield during the previous week meant that the pitch was in excellent condition, though greasy on top, which boded well for a good game. It was hoped that this would facilitate 'the beautiful short passing of the Villa forwards.' (Looker On, *Telegraph*, 8 January 1898) At the same time United could 'give their wings plenty of long passes, although it is not so marked a feature of their play as some metropolitan writers seemed to think.' As kick-off arrived a crowd of 23,887 were inside the ground bringing healthy gate receipts of £602 13s 9d.

First half
Needham lost the toss and United kicked towards the Bramall Lane end. The game

started tentatively but soon the play was of a very high order, as Villa enjoyed the best of the opening exchanges. In fact, after 10 minutes Athersmith had the ball in the net, but fortunately for United it was disallowed.

United seemed to be sparked into action by this and soon began to dominate proceedings. Villa right-back Bowman did well to deny Priest and McKay, but Gaudie then took the ball past him to shoot narrowly wide. United's centre-forward then headed a Priest centre just past the post, while at the other end Thickett dispossessed James Cowan who, after a mazy dribble, was about to shoot.

With two excellent teams on the pitch, it was an outstanding solo effort by Bennett that broke the deadlock after 23 minutes. United's winger received the ball, slipped past Evans, evaded Crabtree's hasty challenge and then closed in on goal to smash the ball past Whitehouse and into the roof of the net, the crowd exploding into enthusiastic cheers.

For five minutes after the goal, the home side were clearly on top, Priest and Cunningham probing the Villa defence in determined and effective style. But the visitors were not about to lie down and after 30 minutes issued a severe warning to United and their fans. Athersmith played a superb ball through to Devey who, just failing to get a touch, saw the ball run on to John Cowan who, in front of an open goal, blasted the ball over the bar. United stormed back. Gaudie touched the ball to Priest who nearly scored with a stinging long shot, while Needham's lob just missed the target. Just before half-time, fine defensive work by Howell and sound goalkeeping by Foulke kept Villa at bay.

Second half

United started brightly, a fine passing move between Cunningham, McKay and Gaudie bringing a good stop out of Whitehouse. The Villa 'keeper then made a fantastic save, flying through the air to keep out a 30-yard screamer from Cunningham. Whitehouse was having a superb game, keeping his side in the match and United at bay, as they attacked strongly over the next few minutes. As Villa finally began to get forward, they found United in stern defensive mood – Thickett and Cain in particularly fine form.

The last 20 minutes saw no relenting in the fast pace of the game, and with just one goal in it both teams were eager for a breakthrough. United thought they had it as a Cain free-kick into the area was hooked goalwards by Gaudie, only for a brilliant diving save from Whitehouse to put the ball round the post. Just before time, Bowman managed to foil Cunningham, who looked like finally adding the second.

Assessment

The Sheffield press were delighted with the victory, especially as the Birmingham press had been a little disparaging about the United team and its style of play. 'Looker On' in the *Telegraph* declared 'Taken throughout there was more than a goal in the play, and United deserved their victory right well.' (*Telegraph*, 17 January 1898)

'Centre-forward' in the *Independent* commended the United players: 'They showed how energy, speed and frequent and accurate shooting, supported by a stout defence, could overcome the so-called scientific combination, pretty passing and dainty finesse which usually broke down at the last moment and fizzled out with a miserable shot in any direction but the right one. What times the mighty Foulke looked on and smiled.' (*Independent*, 17 January 1898)

The Birmingham press had referred to United's half-back line as 'midgets', yet they had held Villa's attack in check while United's forwards had proved potent, their shooting excellent, with the result that Whitehouse, and not Foulke, was kept busy. Special mention was made of Gaudie. Not all observers had felt United's committee had chosen wisely in preferring him to Almond, even though the latter's form had been poor in recent games and he had only just recovered from illness. Gaudie had only played around half a dozen games at centre-forward, and there was clearly room for further improvement: 'though he took the ball beautifully wherever and however it reached him, he passed too slowly to his wings, and seemed a shade upset about the ground. On a dryer one he would do better.' ('Looker On', *Telegraph*, 17 January 1898) Generally, though, he had made a positive contribution. He would continue to set the selection committee a poser at centre-forward in the games to come.

United's victory had given them a clear edge over their rivals and brought them successive victories after two months of indifferent form. Yet although many sections of the national press had United now as champions-elect, local commentators were more circumspect in their assessment. It was noted how the Villa forwards were much stronger at home – United's destination next week. Wolves and West Brom were seen as being in the hunt as were, more importantly, Villa and Everton, referred to as the 'moneyed clubs.' ('Looker On',

Telegraph, 17 January 1898) 'Looker On' was particularly scathing towards such teams and took pride in United's own more parsimonious approach toward the running of the football club, decrying them as 'those to which hundreds are no more than fifties to their rivals, and whose excellences in the field are more due to lavish purchase of their slaves than the cultivation of home talent.' (Ironically both Gaudie and Cunningham would be signed by Villa at the end of the season.)

On completion of the game, Cunningham had a nasty gash across his ankle and Priest was also injured. Fortunately for United, both men would be fit for next week. Having taken tea in the pavilion, the players made their way to Midland Station, where they were cheered off by the delighted crowd of United followers who had gathered to see their heroes. The football committee had decided that they would again be sent to Matlock to train for the return fixture in Birmingham.

Table

		P	W	L	D	Pts
1.	United	19	10	2	7	27
2.	Villa	20	10	6	4	24
3.	Everton	18	9	4	5	23
4.	West Brom	19	8	4	7	23

Other results

Everton 1–0 Wednesday

MATCH NO. 20

ASTON VILLA, AWAY, 15 JANUARY 1898

Result: Aston Villa 1: *Wheldon (pen)*
United 2: *Cunningham (2)*

Half-time: 0–0

Attendance: 43,000 (a record crowd for the Football League), Aston Lower Grounds

Teams:

Aston Villa: Whitehouse, Evans, Bowman, B. Sharpe, James Cowan, Crabtree, Athersmith, Harvey, Devey, Wheldon, Smith.

United: Foulke, Thickett, Cain, Howell, Morren, Needham, Bennett, McKay, Gaudie, Cunningham, Priest.

Referee: Mr John Lewis (Blackburn)

This was clearly going to be a stern test for an unchanged United line up, given that Villa had not yet dropped a point at home. For Villa, John Cowan replaced Smith, a move which strengthened their team given the undoubted class of Cowan, England's brilliant left-winger. United had spent the week in a special training camp at Matlock, while Villa again made several excursions to Droitwich. Again there was massive interest in the contest between the teams. As early as 10am, hundreds were making their way to Aston Lower Grounds and the gates opened early, before noon. Fifteen hundred United fans travelled down on the MS&L railway and found, on their arrival at the ground, that they could only purchase 3/- seats, given the numbers already inside, which were at a good distance from the front. According to the *Telegraph*, 'at two o'clock there must have been 30,000 people on the ground, and the sight on the roads leading thereto was remarkable. When play actually began…hundreds finding a precarious holding on the roof of the unreserved stand and hundreds more being utterly unable to see a single thing that was taking place.' (*Telegraph*, 17 January 1898)

First half

United lost the toss and the game kicked-off at 2.30pm. There was action straight away as Whitehouse fisted away a testing cross by Cunningham and Howell cleared the ball over his own bar. Villa had more of the play but both sides were mounting dangerous attacks. Needham grazed the bar with a shot, while Foulke saved a 'scorcher' from Cowan and Harvey hit the bar for Villa. Bennett then collided with Crabtree and badly twisted his knee. Although lame for a period, he was able to carry on, a crucial bit of good fortune given the injuries sustained by the visitors later in the match.

United began to pass the ball well, and from a corner Morren was provided with a good opportunity but unfortunately shot weakly at Whitehouse. Gaudie then got himself into a shooting position but Evans crashed into him, flooring the United man heavily. With the game halted, 'Gaudie was carried off, the cartilage of his nose being badly misplaced and the player being to all intents and purposes senseless.' (*Telegraph*, 17 January 1898) Against 10 men, Villa now took the initiative and Smith made several fine runs down the left. Injury then struck United again; play stopped with Howell suffering a nasty gash under his eye. Patched up, the half-back continued.

Regardless of their numerical disadvantage, United were unfortunate not to end the half in front. Firstly, McKay hit the post, and then no penalty was forthcoming for the visitors when the referee failed to see Crabtree fist the ball away in Villa's area.

Second half

Ten-men United made a great start, gaining a couple of corners within the opening minute. Unfortunately, Whitehouse was continuing in the rich vein of form he had displayed the previous week. He made two brilliant saves, both from Needham, from United corner-kicks. Unfortunately for United, Bennett seemed lame from his earlier injury and was clearly starting to struggle, though he continued out on the pitch.

With the odds stacking up against them, United fell behind in the 50th minute. Athersmith broke down the right only to be tackled by Cain. The ball, however, broke loose, and as a shot came in Howell handled to keep the ball out of United's goal. A penalty was awarded which Wheldon confidently despatched past Foulke, to tumultuous roars from the massive home crowd.

The goal galvanised United who, putting aside their injury problems, began to stretch the Villa defence. Peppering Whitehouse's goal with shots, Bennett then headed an excellent chance over the bar. Gaudie had now returned to the fray, an exceptionally brave move, regardless of the fact that he clearly did not seem to have much awareness of what was going on.

After Smith had ended a fine run by shooting into United's side netting, the visitors were again denied a penalty. A Needham shot seemed to have been handled by a defender inside the box, but Mr Lewis awarded a free-kick outside. Smith – who was proving a real handful down the left wing, then broke clear and 'drew Foulke almost to the corner flag in very pretty fashion.' (*Telegraph*, 17 January 1898) With United's 'keeper put of position, Smith put an excellent cross into the middle where, fatally, Wheldon hesitated and, before he could get his shot away, was dispossessed – a turning point in the game.

With Needham prompting the United forwards on, it was the visitors who now struck. With only eight minutes left, and most observers feeling Villa would wrap up the win, United suddenly equalised. Howell rushed forward and passed the ball to McKay, who then played it into the Villa area, where Cunningham, racing in, headed the ball past Whitehouse, high up into the net, to tremendous cheers – not just the travelling fans appreciative of the visitors fight back.

The game was now frantic. End-to-end play brought chances for both teams. A goalmouth melee in the Villa area saw a fierce shot by Cunningham somehow kept out, while a misunderstanding between Thickett and Cain let in Wheldon, who was only denied by a sensational save by Foulke. As the game entered the final minute, a draw seemed the obvious result, but United were not finished. Gaudie, Priest and Cunningham combined, with the latter bearing down on goal when Villa's Bowman challenged him, only to fall on the floor, leaving the ball uncleared – ' 'ere he had a chance of recovering himself, the ball was at Cunningham's toe and sped into the net before the crowd had realised the possibility of another goal.' (*Telegraph*, 17 January 1898)

With the whistle blown, United had won, their efforts under difficult circumstances recognised by many in the crowd who cheered the victors loudly. Gaudie practically collapsed as the game ended; the Villa players were stunned that victory, which seemed so certain with only eight minutes to go, had been snatched from them. To the credit of the home players, Percy Young notes how 'at the end the United were cheered from the field by a sporting Villa team, who thus asserted the natural aristocracy of their tradition.'

Assessments

Ernest Needham, recalling the game later, wrote 'The greatest interest was taken in the match, especially after the last week's result, for there was a general opinion that it would decide who would be champion for the season. Luck seemed against us early in the game, and we soon lost the services of our centre-forward, who retired with a broken nose. He did not return until 10 minutes from the finish, and then the Villans were leading by one to none. But this was Cunningham's day, and he showed it by scoring two goals in the last three [eight] minutes. What a sensation finish!' (*Association Football*)

Needham himself had had a magnificent game and William McGregor, founder of the Football League, noted United's 'all round excellence. No player, unless it be Needham, overshadowing another.' Like the Sheffield press the week before, McGregor also rebuked the Birmingham newspapers, who had scoffed at United's half-back line – 'the midgets' – declaring that they were 'unequalled as a trio by any other team in England.'

The Birmingham papers, having seen United win twice against their favourites, were now more ready to accord them some respect, although insisting, as was the belief nationally, that their strength lay in their team spirit and organisation, rather than in the individual brilliance of the players, an assessment perhaps unfair on many within the team.

The *Birmingham Mail* declared 'Individually they are nothing exceptional; collectively they are a magnificent combination. Each man seemed to know intuitively today where a colleague was...the visitors did not trouble about finesse or fine points; they had come to Villa Park to get goals if they possibly could, and they meant having them.'

The *Birmingham Gazette* noted 'The Sheffielders are a wonderfully balanced team, for with, perhaps, the exception of Needham, there is no player of striking brilliance.'

Nationally, the *Morning Leader* picked up on the tenacity of the United players in overcoming the difficulties they suffered with injuries during the game. It was a point that was picked up by many of the 'Nationals': 'If only for their magnificent pluck and indomitable wearing down energy the Blades ought to have won. It was superior stamina rather than skill which robbed the Birmingham eleven of honours.'

The reference to superior stamina was also reflected in 'Looker-On's' assessment in the *Telegraph*, who believed it was their special training at Matlock which had given them the edge over the Villa players: 'training has unquestionably done much for the Sheffielders, and, while the Villa were beaten at all points in the last quarter of an hour, it was superiority in point of condition which was responsible for this…a magnificent tribute to George Waller's efforts.'

In terms of their play, 'centre-forward' in the *Independent* proudly declared that United 'have never done anything better than they did on Saturday at Villa Park.' 'Looker-On' added 'That the United men deserved their victory is a fact which few people will be inclined to dispute who saw the game.' All the players were roundly praised by the two Sheffield papers, with Needham, as nationally, seen as United's star man. It was generally felt that Needham, the England international, and Villa's Scottish international James Cowan had been giants on the field of play. Most of all, the game had been a magnificent spectacle. It had taken place before a magnificent crowd; the stands full, supporters perched on top, 'truly it was a fine sight, the like of which has never been seen at a football match. The game was worthy of the crowd' recorded the *Birmingham Daily Post*.

For the travelling supporters it was a fantastic occasion, and once the victory was secured the celebrations quickly ensued. 'Every excursionist had decided that defeat would have to be put up with when the goals came, and with them an enthusiasm which lasted all the way back to Birmingham, thence to Sheffield, and which even at the Midland Station here broke out repeatedly.' (*Telegraph*, 17 January 1898)

The fans back home in Sheffield were also delighted with the news of the victory, and even though the team's train arrived back late at Midland Station at 9.45pm ' 'ere it steamed in, fully 500 cheers went up from full 500 throats, and the reception was a royal one.' (*Telegraph*, 17 January 1898)

Cheered up by their victory and their fans enthusiasm, the players had another reason to be happy. The team had decided to let their playing bonuses accumulate until the end of the season. With the win at Villa, there was well over £100 in the kitty so far.

Table

		P	W	L	D	Pts
1.	United	20	11	2	7	29
2.	West Brom	20	9	4	7	25
3.	Sunderland	20	10	6	4	24
4.	Aston Villa	21	10	7	4	24

Other results

West Brom 3–1 Preston

Sunderland 2–1 Bury

With their second defeat to United, Villa now effectively slipped out of the title race. However, a new rival was beginning to emerge. After a shaky start to the season, Sunderland were beginning to hit a run of form and had come quietly up on the rails into third place.

MATCH No. 21

WOLVES, HOME, 22 JANUARY 1898

Result: United 2: *Almond, McKay*
            Wolves 1: *Smith*

Half-time: 1–0
Attendance: 11,500

Teams:
United: Foulke, Thickett, Cain, Howell, Morren, Needham, Bennett, McKay,
            Almond, Cunningham, Priest.
Wolves: Baddaley, Eccles, Blackett, Griffiths, Malpass, Fleming, Tonks, Wood,
            Beats, Smith, Miller.

Referee: Mr A. Scragg (Crewe)

Due to Gaudie's injury, Almond was brought back at centre-forward. Pleased with United's performances against Aston Villa, the football committee kept the team in special training at Chesterfield House at Matlock Bank for the week prior to the game.

First half
United lost the toss and were forced by the visitors to face into the sun. It did not have much of an effect though as within a minute the home side were in front. Beats handled and United were awarded a free-kick; Cain delivered and Almond, on his return to the side, headed home.

With United's half-back line carrying on their good form from the previous week, the Wolves forwards were finding it hard to make any progress, although the visitors did have the ball in the net from an indirect free-kick, but it was disallowed by the referee as no second player touched the ball. United then had two good opportunities to go further ahead. From a corner, Needham skimmed the top of the bar and a Bennett shot from out on the right almost beat Baddaley.

As the game moved into the second quarter, Wolves finally began to exert some pressure and Foulke had to be alert, making several clearances. Thickett was then kicked in the stomach and had to be carried off, meaning United were forced to play the rest of the half with 10 men. Re-organising, Needham moved to right-back and Priest took over 'Nudger's' position at left-half. Encouraged by their numerical advantage, Wolves now had a sustained period of pressure. With Foulke making some good saves from Wood, among others, United reached half-time a goal to the good.

Second half

Thickett returned with the rest of the United players and was greeted with a great cheer from the crowd. The game was very competitive and both teams were creating chances. Cain scored from an indirect free-kick, but, like Wolves in the first half, it went directly into the net and was disallowed by the referee. At the other end Miller raced away and crossed to Beats, 'but Foulke fisted away with a huge lunge.' United's 'keeper then kept out a dangerous Miller cross as Wolves began to apply a lot of pressure. In danger of losing their lead, United finally turned the tables. Gaining a corner, Priest took it short to Needham, who centred it and McKay, running on to it, put the ball past Baddaley 'amid a scene of the wildest enthusiasm'. United now had a cushion, which was important as Wolves came back into the game when Smith, moving onto a throw in, crashed an unstoppable shot past Foulke.

With no further scoring, United were able to claim their fourth successive win.

Assessments

It had been a close and tough game. United had not played brilliantly but had scored two good goals and both their full-backs had been carrying injuries. Thickett had missed the latter part of the first half and Cain had been charged fiercely in the second, with the result that after the game he was found to have two broken ribs. Wolves had certainly been physical, they were 'decidedly vigorous and there was plenty of what is known as "playing the man"'. (*Telegraph*, 24 January 1898)

However, their forwards, after a shaky start, had shown up more than United's and Bennett had been particularly shackled by young left-back Blackett.

Table

		P	W	L	D	Pts
1.	United	21	12	2	7	31
2.	Sunderland	21	11	6	4	26
3.	West Brom	20	9	4	7	25
4.	Everton	20	9	5	6	24
5.	Aston Villa	22	10	8	4	24

Other results

Sunderland 1–0 Liverpool

Derby 3–1 Aston Villa

MATCH NO. 22

LIVERPOOL, AWAY, 5 FEBRUARY 1898

Result: Liverpool 0

United 4: *Cunningham, Logan (2), Johnson*

Half-time: 0–1

Attendance: 17,500, Anfield

Teams:

Liverpool: Storer, Goldie, Dunlop, McCartney, McQue, Cleghorn, Geary, McCowie, Hartley, Berton, Bradshaw.

United: Foulke, Thickett, Cain, Johnson, Morren, Needham, Bennett, McKay, Cunningham, Logan, Priest.

Referee: Mr T. Armitt (Leeds)

United's line up saw Johnson in to replace Howell, who was suffering from a 'leg strain', and with both Gaudie and Almond injured, Neil Logan continued at centre-forward, having represented the first team on the previous Wednesday in the FA Cup at Burslem Port Vale. United's defeat in the first-round replay against a non-League side had shocked supporters and led to much criticism. There were those who tried to put a positive aspect on the Cup knock out, declaring, as managers do today, that the defeat would allow the team to concentrate on the League; the Championship being a far greater prize. However, this ignored the fact that Preston and Aston Villa had already done the double. Yet the club was aware that criticism of the players would not be slow to emerge should there be a dip in form. A definite positive for United was that Bob Cain, out injured for both of the Cup games, was able to resume his place in the side.

Of further interest was the *Telegraph's* report that, following the game, a representative of the new Football Players' Union, a man called Somerville, would be interviewing the United players with a view to them joining up; only they and the Wednesday players of the key League clubs had still to commit themselves. The

Telegraph noted that 'last week it was virtually settled that Needham and his men should agree to take up membership of the Union' and, perhaps surprisingly, the newspaper declared itself supportive of the move – firmly believing that the current transfer and wage bargaining systems were unfair on the players.

At any rate, the players could not claim that the United football committee were not eager to support their title ambitions, as the team was once again sent to Matlock during the week to continue with their special training. The fans were still showing a willingness to follow the team away and a few hundred made their way to Liverpool.

The Match

In greasy conditions, Liverpool won the toss, kicked-off and started the brighter. There were two early opportunities for Hartley, but firstly he was dispossessed by Cain and lost out again as he dallied too long on the ball before shooting. Geary then hit the post for the home side before United got into gear – a slick passing move between McKay and Bennett leading to the right-winger crossing the ball to Needham, who struck the bar with a firm shot. This was the signal for the visitors to take the initiative and Liverpool only just managed to survive a series of attacks.

Unfortunately for Bennett, the winger was badly fouled by Dunlop and was 'eventually compelled to retire, suffering great agony'. (*Telegraph*, 7 February 1898) Yet with only 10 men, United continued to hold their own and almost took the lead as Priest shot just over the bar following a Cain free-kick. Following treatment, Bennett returned to the pitch and, though not at his full potential, still managed to send in a fine shot which had the Liverpool 'keeper, Storer, in difficulties.

Playing with some skill and confidence, United got the breakthrough. A fine passing move involving Needham, Priest, Cunningham and Logan saw the ball return to Cunningham, who beat Storer with a fine shot, the *Telegraph* reporter noting that 'the Sheffielders on the ground naturally went wild with delight.'

Bennett was clearly felt aggrieved with Dunlop for the injury inflicted upon him by the Liverpool full-back. Since his return to the field of play, he had been carrying on a running battle with his opponent. Finally, matters between the two came to a head: 'at length the Sheffielder crashed into the Liverpudlian, the result being…[Dunlop] had to be helped from the field.' Roundly booed by the home supporters, Bennett was defended by the *Telegraph's* reporter, who took Bennett's 'treatment' as a sound, moral lesson for the Liverpool man. Commenting on the

Liverpool fans boos the reporter declared: 'for this there was no necessity as either player was as bad as the other, and Dunlop, as the aggressor, got no more than his desserts.' No condemnation for justifiable retaliation in the sporting Victorian age.

Second half

As the second half commenced, Dunlop had reappeared, heartily cheered by the home supporters. It did not take long, however, for United to extend their lead. Logan, out on the right, cut in and shot powerfully at the Liverpool goal. Storer made a good save, diving to push the ball away. Unfortunately for the Liverpool 'keeper, the ball was played back across the area and Logan, rushing in, knocked the ball in before Storer could recover.

From this point on, the visitors were never in any danger of losing their grip on the game. United's half-back line were expertly containing Liverpool's attacks and their forwards were creating plenty of problems for the home defence. It was hardly surprising that United scored again, but the source of the goal perhaps was. When Johnson dispossessed Bradshaw and advanced on the Liverpool goal, he was tripped. Taking the free-kick himself, the ball was blocked by Berton. Rebounding to Johnson, the United man lashed at the ball, which flew obliquely through the ruck of players and passed Storer into the net. It was Johnson's first League goal for the club.

With the heart gone from the Liverpool team, United added a fourth. Following a free-kick into the area, there was a scramble on the Liverpool goalline, Logan applied the final touch as the ball entered the net. With that, the Liverpool fans headed for the exits.

Assessment

United had been vastly superior to their opponents and had gained revenge for the defeat inflicted on them at the Lane in late December. Logan had done well but was not seen as a perfect deputy for Almond or Gaudie: 'would be more useful if he was 5 or 6 yards faster'. (Looker On, *Telegraph*, 7 February 1898) The way in which the team had got over the defeat was pleasing, just three days earlier, in the Cup. The club was especially delighted, as it diffused the criticism that was threatening to build around the players, and they later declared 'there never was a neater or more effectual answer to the cries that Burslem had foretold our collapse, that henceforward our dreams of championship were at an end.'

However, if it was believed that United could finally put the Burslem game behind them, such views proved incorrect. The *Telegraph* was still irritated by the defeat and after the Liverpool game was focusing on the incompetence of the referee in the Port Vale tie, Mr Cooper, who had insisted United play extra-time in the game when the players had stated they did not wish to. Precedents in last season's ties (Bolton and Grimsby; Preston and Villa) had established their right to do this. Additionally, Vale had scored as Foulke had left his goal to join in the United attacks and was caught out by a quick counter. Yet the goal was, according to most commentators, offside, and again the referee had let United down. Although it seemed the local press were trying to defend the team, in reality they were keeping the Cup tie at the forefront of the supporters' minds, and when United again hit a sticky patch it was another key incident with which to criticise the players.

Table

		P	W	L	D	Pts
1.	United	22	13	2	7	33
2.	Sunderland	22	12	6	4	28
3.	West Brom	21	10	4	7	27
4.	Aston Villa	23	11	8	4	26

Other results

Sunderland 1–0 Notts County
West Brom 3–1 Blackburn
Aston Villa 4–0 Preston

MATCH NO. 23

BOLTON, HOME, 7 FEBRUARY 1898

Result: United 4: *Priest, Logan (2), Bennett*

Bolton 0

Half-time: 1–0
Attendance: 5,000

Teams:

United: Foulke, Thickett, Cain, Johnson, Morren, Needham, Bennett, McKay, Logan, Cunningham, Priest.

Bolton: Sutcliffe, Somerville, Davies, Paton, Brown, Freebairn, Cassidy, Gilligan, T. Miller, Wright, Jack.

Referee: Mr F. Townsend (Walsall)

United were unchanged from their victory at Liverpool. Although Bolton were near the bottom of the table, a tough game was expected as the visitors had entered on a good run of form, a recent Cup victory at Luton indicative of this. Although it was a Monday fixture, there was disappointment that United had only drawn a crowd of 5,000.

First half

With Needham losing the toss, United were forced to play into the sun and for the first five minutes struggled as the visitors seized the initiative. Foulke made a good save from Wright and Gilligan missed a straightforward chance. United then got into their stride as both sides attacked with conviction, seeking the opening goal. It was United who got it. After 17 minutes, Bennett lobbed the ball into the area and Priest, running in, met it and diverted it past Sutcliffe and into the net.

The goal signalled a period of United dominance. Johnson had two excellent shots – clearly inspired by his debut strike at Liverpool – the first just saved by Sutcliffe; the second just over the bar. Priest then dribbled through the Bolton defence but, with only Sutcliffe to beat, shot wide. Pulling themselves together, Bolton hit back. Foulke made two good saves following a Wanderers' corner, but then Sutcliffe was forced into another good stop from Priest. Just before half-time, Bolton gained a corner and from it were unfortunate to hit the post.

Second half

With the warning given to them by the visitors just before half-time, United began the second half in determined fashion and were soon two goals in front. Sutcliffe was unable to gather in a cross from the left, and Logan was on hand to tap the ball home. From the restart, United gained possession and Needham, out on the left, sent in an excellent cross, which Bennett, running on to, shot past a stunned Sutcliffe.

United remained on top and it was not surprising that a fourth goal came. Clever, tricky play by McKay ended in the Scot feeding the ball to Logan, who sent in an angled shot past the Bolton 'keeper.

Towards the end Bolton had a couple of chances to score, but both Jack and Gilligan failed to beat Foulke. United had their second successive 4–0 win and clearly deserved this home victory.

Assessment

With Logan scoring twice in successive games, 'Looker On' had somewhat reversed his opinion of the young centre-forward, following his reservations after the Liverpool game. The 19-year-old player, almost six feet in height and hailing from Blantyre, was now a player of real promise 'With all the prospects of filling out into a really well built athlete.' (*Telegraph*, 8 February 1898)

More significant was the developing form of Harry Johnson, who had performed consistently well deputising along the half-back line during the season; 'he has played a couple of wonderfully good games for his club this few games in place of Howell. Size he has in plenty and speed as well. Now and then he was beaten for lack of experience, but he will get better at that and…will develop into a real class man'.

The view of 'Looker On' was shared by the club who also observed 'how well Morren plays just now with Johnson, stout hearted and clever in Howell's place on the right.' (Programme, *Reserves versus Black Watch*, 12 February 1898) In all probability, it was the emergence of the Ecclesfield man that made the football committee willing to sell Howell later in the season.

Table

		P	W	L	D	Pts
1.	United	23	14	2	7	35
2.	Sunderland	22	12	6	4	28
3.	West Brom	21	10	4	7	27
4.	Aston Villa	23	11	8	4	26

No other games played.

MATCH NO. 24

NOTTS COUNTY, HOME, 19 FEBRUARY 1898

Result: United 0

             Notts County 1: *Murphy*

Half-time: 0–1

Attendance: 8,500

Teams:

United: Foulke, Thickett, Cain, Howell, Morren, Needham, Bennett, McKay, Logan, Cunningham, Priest.

Notts County: Toone, Lewis, Prescott, Steward, Calderhead, Bull, Fraser, Boucher, Murphy, Carter, Langham.

Referee: Unknown

Playing against the bottom club, who they had defeated 3–1 in Nottingham on New Year's Day, United were expected to win easily. Nevertheless, a 'fair number' of County supporters had travelled to Sheffield hoping that their favourites could take something from the game. United made one change. Howell, now fully recovered, was brought back in place of Johnson.

First half

Needham won the toss and decided to attack the Shoreham Street end. Play was scrappy to begin with, the first real chance falling to County's Boucher, who sent in a 'stinging shot' which was saved by Foulke. Responding, United had two good shots by Morren and then Bennett, both of which were well saved by Toone.

    After these early exchanges it was the visitors who went ahead, the goal 'one of the prettiest little comedies it has ever been our lot to witness on a football field.' (*Telegraph*, 21 February 1898) Carter outwitted Thickett on the left and pushed the ball past him. Foulke, believing he could reach it first, raced out, but found Carter too quick for him, the County man dodging past him to the right. Cain rushing in would surely clear the ball – but somehow missed it. With the ball running clear, Langham raced in facing an open goal. The winger contrived to hit the post, but fortunately for the visitors Murphy, following up, made no mistake from the rebound.

With the lead, the County defence set themselves for the inevitable United assault. Well marshalled by Calderhead, they efficiently kept the home side at bay until half-time.

Second half

County had now clearly set themselves into defensive mode, intent on holding on to what they had – 'content to play a waiting game, acting chiefly on the defensive and exhibiting no hurry about it.'

Frustrated, the home side had much of the play but spent the rest of the game unable to create any real goalscoring opportunities. The result was that United went down to their second home defeat of the season.

Assessment

Both main Sheffield newspapers showed extreme disappointment at the defeat. The *Independent's* 'Centre-Forward' declared that it was a performance 'calculated to irritate and disappoint their faithful friends and followers' while 'Looker On' in the *Telegraph* noted that too often United's home performances had been poor: 'Inexplicably poor form which they have time after time shown in front of their own supporters, again turned up'. Although 'Centre-Forward' credited the County defence, 'it is scarcely possible to pay a higher compliment to the defensive play of Calderhead and his comrades', the United forwards had lacked creativity and, as 'Looker-On' observed, their play 'seldom rose above the low level of mediocrity.'

The defeat quickly resurrected memories of the recent Cup reversal, United's performance being likened by 'Centre-Forward' to 'the dismal English Cup tie collapse at Burslem.' National assessments were no different. 'Pearson's Record' declaring 'Notts deserved their victory, for they showed a dash which, while lacking finished play, certainly put the United's dismally doleful efforts completely into the shade. The Sheffield team has not made such another wretched exhibition this season.'

More importantly, because the team, and many of its individual players, had set such high standards during the season, crowd expectations were now at such a level that any drop in performance was likely to result in vocal criticism from the terraces. Walter Bennett, in particular, was such a target, it being felt that his recent form was disappointing. In fact, the football committee decided before the next game at home to Everton that Bennett should be rested. Rather than showing sympathy for the player, the *Telegraph* reported 'it comes as no surprise that Bennett had been dropped for the match against Everton tomorrow'. The late Victorian Press, like their contemporaries today, were quite prepared to 'build them up and knock them down' when it came to their footballing heroes.

The football committee were also concerned about United's failures at home, but they believed that much of the problem was due to the enormous pressure that was being exerted on the players; that the supporters had to provide them with encouragement, not criticism, if they were to perform at their best:

'We all feel the disappointment and so do the players, who are unanimous that it would be better to play the whole of their matches out of town, because they say the public scoff and jeer their play to such an extent they lose their verve and vigour…Let Burslem rest; it is a matter of history. And for the present and future lies buried.'

Table

		P	W	L	D	Pts
1.	United	24	14	3	7	35
2.	Sunderland	23	12	6	5	29
3.	West Brom	22	10	4	8	28
4.	Wednesday	24	12	9	3	27

Other results

West Brom 2–2 Sunderland
Wednesday 2–1 Derby

Following the game the players again went away to Matlock for special training, due to return in three days time for the Everton game.

MATCH NO. 25

EVERTON, HOME, 19 FEBRUARY 1898

Result: United 0
             Everton 0

Half-time: 0–0
Attendance: 9,500

Teams:

United: Foulke, Thickett, Cain, Howell, Morren, Needham, Gaudie, McKay,
           Logan, Cunningham, Priest.
Everton: Muir, Balmer, Storrier, Stewart, Holt, Robertson, Taylor, Divers,
           Cameron, Chadwick, Bell.

Referee: Mr J.H. Strawson (Lincoln)

United made one change for the Tuesday game, one that was to arouse an element
of controversy. Bennett was dropped in place of Gaudie, now recovered, who took
over on the right wing, rather than at centre-forward, where Logan continued. The
early assumptions were that Bennett was being rested, as his form had not been so
good of late and he was becoming a target for the 'boo boys' among the home
crowd. Rumours then emerged that Bennett had fallen into dispute with the football
committee and wished to leave the club. The committee quickly moved to scotch the
rumours in the Everton match programme. Interestingly, in doing so the
committee's comments indicate to the modern observer the nature of the class
system of the day. They show the way in which working-class professionals were
regarded by the directors and officials of their clubs. The latter regarded themselves
as the players' social superiors and 'masters'. Stating that Bennett had been rested as
he was clearly out of sorts, the 'official' line continued:

'The rumours about him being dissatisfied with his masters is all "tommy rot".
It is not for us to brag about our masters, but there is not one of the players but who
has the highest praise for them; and we think the sharp progress from the start right

up to today is due to the splendid feeling existing between the players and the committee.'

First half

A period of bright sunshine had resulted in the hard pitch being thawed on top, which created a treacherous, greasy surface that made it extremely difficult for both sides to perform to their capabilities.

Perhaps because of the appeals of the United committee, or the realisation that the team still had a Championship to win and the crowd had to play their part, the home fans got behind the team throughout the game and 'gave their favourites all the encouragement that powerful lungs could afford.' (*Telegraph*, 23 February 1898)

Needham won the toss and kicked towards the Bramall Lane end and into the sun. There was an early chance for Everton's Taylor, but Foulke saved. Gaudie then shot into Muir's hands, the 'keeper following this by turning a Logan effort away for a corner. From the resultant kick the ball fell to the Everton forward Bell, who proceeded to run the full length of the pitch only for Howell to clear his final shot.

United responded with a period of sustained pressure. In a series of goalmouth scrambles, Muir made three fine saves. From a corner, Morren headed goalwards, only to see his effort cleared off the line by Balmer. Unable to find the breakthrough, United had defending of their own to do as Everton came back into the game. Chances were now being created at both ends of the field. As half-time approached, the playing conditions were getting worse, both sides finding it increasingly difficult to get a sure footing on the greasy ground.

Second half

There was lots of hard work from both sides, but the conditions made it difficult to create clear openings. United switched Gaudie with Logan, hoping the former would have more impact in the centre. There were attempts on goal: Taylor shot wide for Everton and Priest for United. Gaudie, moving wide, passed in to Logan, who headed beyond the post. Everton thought they would score as Bell ran through on Foulke, but the United 'keeper pulled off a good save. The final opportunity fell to McKay, whose shot was well saved by Muir, the game ending in a goalless draw.

Assessment

The conditions had not favoured either team, but at least, following the disappointing performance against Notts County, United had played well and did provide opportunities to break the deadlock, especially in the first half. Most satisfying was the way in which the supporters had rallied behind the players and it was to be hoped that the club could now remain 'United' until the end of the season.

Table

		P	W	L	D	Pts
1.	United	25	14	3	8	36
2.	Sunderland	24	13	6	5	31
3.	West Brom	22	10	4	8	28
4.	Wednesday	24	12	9	3	27

Other results

Sunderland 2–0 Bolton

MATCH NO. 26

SUNDERLAND, AWAY, 5 MARCH 1898

Result: Sunderland 3: *Wilson, Howell (og 2)*
            United 1: *Cunningham*

Half-time: 1–1
Attendance: 23,500, Roker Park

Teams:
Sunderland: Doig, Bach, Boyle, Ferguson, McAlister, Dunlop, Morgan, Leslie,
            Brown, Wilson, Saxton.
United: Foulke, Thickett, Cain, Howell, Johnson, Needham, Bennett, McKay,
            Gaudie, Cunningham, Priest.

Referee: Mr Rollins (Walsall)

With Morren on international duty for Ireland in Belfast, Johnson was brought in at centre-half, while Bennett returned to the right wing and Gaudie replaced Logan at centre-forward. The concern over a free-scoring centre-forward had never been far below the surface all season, and although both Almond and Gaudie had done reasonably well neither were considered the finished article. The match programme for the friendly against Wednesday on the previous Saturday clearly alluded to this problem by highlighting the capabilities of the club's first key centre-forward, Harry Hammond:

'Harry Hammond's scoring proclivities would just help us upwards to the final. We could do with such a scorer as he was in the early days of 1892. During the months of September and October Hammond, Dobson and Watson scored over 40 goals – fancy that now.' (It should have been noted that this was in a lower standard of football.)

With United heading the table, the programme also carried an article entitled 'A Retrospect, and our future prospects.' In this, the football committee outlined the philosophy that had driven the development of the club to its present point.

SHEFFIELD UNITED.

RIGHT WING.   Goal :   LEFT WING.
                           Foulkes.

                           Backs :
        Thickett.   Cain.

                           Half-Backs :
        Howell   Morren.   Needham.

                           Forwards :
Bennett.   McKay.   Gaudie.   Cunningham   Priest.
                                        (or Almond).

            Referee :—Mr. A. KINGSCOTT, of Derby.

                           Forwards :
Henderson.   McMahon.   Allan.   Campbell.   Gilhooly.

                           Half-Backs :
        King.   Russey.   Goldie.

                           Backs :
        Doyle.   Welford.
                           Goal :
LEFT WING.   McArthur.   RIGHT WING.

CELTIC.

Sheffield United line up against Celtic in a 'Battle of Britain' exhibition match, 12 March 1898.

Contemporary readers may find it of interest in the sense that it reflects a similar approach to that taken by the current board of directors:

'We have studiously avoided bringing in big priced men, because if we had done so we should have had a large adverse balance at the present time. We have also endeavoured to get youth, believing "that a good young 'un is better than a good old 'un." We have put up two good stands and made other arrangements on the ground which we think the public have appreciated. Certainly we have catered for the majority and nowhere in England can the "sixpenny spectator" be accommodated so well as at Bramall Lane. Now we should like…to buy outright Bramall Lane.'

Combined with the comments made in the aftermath of the victory over Aston Villa at the Lane, it was clear that United were never to be one of the 'big' clubs in terms of having unlimited financial resources, but clearly in a very 'sporting' age United's way of combining parsimony with the development of home-grown talent was seen as most commendable.

The games against Sunderland – United had to face them at the Lane, two League games hence – were now going to be the key to the Championship. The Wearsiders, after a shaky start, had been in excellent form of late and lay in second place, five points behind United with a game in hand. If United were to lose both matches then there was a good chance that they could be pipped to the title.

The game had generated huge interest on Wearside, and by kick-off a record crowd of 23,500 were in the ground – a fact that was to cause major problems and lead to huge controversy over the final outcome of the game. Basically, there were too many people in the ground well before the game began, but with record receipts of over £800 the Sunderland directors were not too concerned. The United changing room roof was wrecked by a number of spectators using it as a vantage point. Given the crush, there was no option but to allow spectators to sit between the barriers around the pitch. This led to thousands of people racing across the ground just before the game started, in order to get a better view. When the teams took to the field, spectators were pressed up against the touchlines on all sides of the ground and right up to the goal posts. Furthermore, the United players were greeted by a very hostile and intimidating crowd as they came out.

First half

Needham lost the toss and United were asked to defend the lower goal. The match was, as expected, hotly contested from the start, with both sides having chances in the early period. It was Sunderland who went in front, in very unfortunate circumstances for United and right-half Rab Howell – for whom the game was to be a personal disaster. After nine minutes Morgan put in a cross that seemed to be clearly heading beyond the far post. With no Sunderland attacker threatening, Howell inexplicably diverted the ball into the net, giving Foulke absolutely no chance.

To United's credit, they shook off their misfortune and, ignoring the wild exuberance of the home supporters, continued to attack their opponents. Gaudie was just wide with a smart shot, Cunningham dribbled through but fired over the bar with only Doig to beat and a good move almost got Gaudie in again, but for a great challenge by Boyle. Perhaps United were a little too eager: 'Over anxiety seemed to be spoiling the Sheffielders, whose mid-field work was very clever and attractive.' (*Telegraph*, 7 March 1898)

United were still playing well and creating chances. Bennett shot into the side netting and Boyle headed Cunningham's shot off the line, with Doig beaten. Yet the Sheffield men were not to be denied, and on 40 minutes they finally equalised. A Bennett shot was cleared out to Howell who, making up for his earlier error, played a good cross in to Cunningham who headed it home, a goal 'greeted with almost perfect silence.'

Second half

Problems with the crowd encroaching on to the pitch meant that the referee was forced to delay the restart. Whether this unnerved the United players is not certain, but straight from the kick-off Wilson gained the ball and set off on a mazy dribble that ended in him firing home a superb goal in off the post. Disappointingly, only Needham had threatened to dispossess him as he ran through. United tried to get back into the game and both Priest and Cunningham threatened the home defence. Sunderland, however, were fired up and began to exert further pressure. On 63 minutes they were 3–1 up. Morgan got away, knocked in a cross that was heading straight to Foulke, only for Howell to once again divert the ball into his own net.

United did not give up and worked hard to get something from the game. Bennett, taking a pass from Gaudie, outwitted Boyle and put an excellent cross into the area, which Priest, racing in, was just unable to get a touch to. Bennett then dribbled through again setting up Howell, who just missed with a shot. Before the end Howell had a shot cleared off the line and Johnson, with a good opening, shot over. Throwing caution to the wind, United left themselves open to the counter-attack but fortunately Sunderland were unable to extend their lead further.

Assessment

In their own assessment of the game, the United committee tried to be as objective as possible, not wanting it to appear that they were looking at the serious crowd problems as an excuse for the team's defeat. Their views were transmitted to the fans in an article entitled 'Saturday at Sunderland' in the Celtic programme of 12 March: 'One of the saddest days in our 1898 experience! We went to Roker on Friday night well and hearty – all right in point of health, for a splendid struggle, and full of hope; but we went under, beaten by a couple of goals, put through our own goal by one of our side. Howell has been one of the best of our half-backs for years past; it was his day of misfortune on Saturday last. Really, on the play in the first half, we ought to have won with ease. Our passing uphill and against the sun was as accurate as possible and full of dash and fire, and when we crossed over at the intervals with the scores level it looked just about as good a thing as could be wished.'

The team were unable to push on, in the club's opinion, for one main reason: 'nothing but the state of the crowds, hanging all over the touchlines, lost us the most important match'.

Consequently, United had lodged a protest with the League against the result, noting that this was not a selfish act but was 'not only in our own interest, but in those of the game'. Unfortunately for United, the appeal was to be turned down by the League and created further acrimony between themselves and Sunderland.

But was United's view of the situation shared by the press? Not surprisingly, the Sheffield papers agreed with the club, backing its decision to appeal. 'Looker On' in the *Telegraph* placed the blame squarely on the shoulders of the Sunderland committee, who had caused the severe overcrowding by 'their anxiety to secure the uttermost sixpence' and pointed out that four times the referee had been forced to stop the play due to encroachments of supporters on to the pitch. Furthermore, fans had interfered with United's wingers, had got in their way when tackling corners and even passed in front of Foulke during the game.

Outside Sheffield, there was more emphasis placed on the performance of the players, and it was felt that weaknesses in the team had undermined their chance of victory. Morren's absence was particularly highlighted, it being felt that he would have held the half-back line together better and would have tackled Wilson to stop the second Sunderland goal. In addition, Johnson had not seemed as alert as usual, and Howell's performance had been well below his usual standards. While Priest and Bennett had played well on the wings, support in the centre had been poor, particularly in the second half, and chances had not been taken effectively. The concern about United's goalscoring was also restated in the Celtic programme: 'We want goals getting in our League matches. The recent games don't look very promising.' It should be noted that the general consensus was that Foulke had again played well, the United custodian proving to be a bright spark in the team throughout the season.

Sunderland, it was acknowledged, were a fine side, a point accepted by the Sheffield papers too. They were on a tremendous run and had won nine and drawn one of their last 10 League games. In the game, Morgan had shown himself a clever right-winger, Saxton had been effective on the left, Wilson had worked extremely hard and Dunlop had been excellent in the air. Concerned that United's players needed freshening up, 'Looker On' proffered some advice to the United committee: 'I should stop special training for a time if I were the committee and let the men "run loose" for a day or two. Staleness is one of the most fatal diseases footballers can suffer from.'

Trying to keep positive, the club reassured people not to panic. Recognising that these were indeed nervous times and two tough games were coming up against West Brom and Sunderland, the committee declared 'There is no real reason why we should not win the Championship even yet. We have given our friends a bit of a shock but there's nothing actually wrong yet.' (Celtic programme)

Table

		P	W	L	D	Pts
1.	United	26	14	4	8	36
2.	Sunderland	25	14	6	5	33
3.	Wednesday	25	13	9	3	29
4.	West Brom	22	10	4	8	28

Other results

Wednesday 2–0 Wolves

The following week United had no League game and Sunderland won their game in hand to go just one point behind them.

MATCH NO. 27

WEST BROM, AWAY, 26 MARCH 1898

Result: West Brom 2: *Garfield, Richards*
United 0

Half-time: 1–0
Attendance: 4,200, Stoney Lane

Teams:

West Brom: Reader, Cave, Williams, Perry, Jones, Banks, Bassett, Connor, Richards, McKenzie, Garfield.

United: Foulke, Thickett, Cain, Howell, Logan, Needham, Bennett, McKay, Hedley, Cunningham, Priest.

Referee: Unknown

It was three weeks since the Sunderland game, and United had spent the previous two Saturdays playing a fixture at home to Celtic, the first part of an unofficial Championship of Great Britain, and then visiting London to play in the first ever Charity Shield fixture against Corinthians – the game billed as the top professional side against the top amateur one. For the West Brom game, United moved Logan back to play in the half-back line, given the unavailability of Morren and Gaudie, while George Hedley was given his debut at centre-forward. United were again forced to play a fixture in adverse weather conditions – a 'hurricane' blowing from start to finish, accompanied by snow – and this also affected the size of the crowd, with just over 4,000 attending.

First half

Given the difficult conditions, the play was frantic and few real chances were created. The home team did make the early running and Garfield sent in a rasping shot that was just wide, then the same player, set up by Connor, hesitated in front of goal and Foulke was able to clear.

United then began to mount attacks of their own. Priest was set up by Hedley, his curling shot taken round the post by the wind. A minute later Hedley's effort flashed across the goal and then Bennett got in a shot but was offside. Hitting back, a good passing move by the Albion forwards led to a fierce shot which was well saved by Foulke. It was a warning to the United defence and just before half-time the home team did go in front, Garfield heading the ball past Foulke into the far corner of the net. On top, Albion nearly added to their lead before the break. Garfield outpaced Howell and shot just wide, while Foulke made an excellent save with three Albion forwards advancing on him.

Second half

Foulke was immediately called on, making a brilliant left-handed save from a Richards shot and, given that Albion clearly now had the advantage of the wind gusting strongly down the pitch, it looked as if United would be in for a difficult and testing time. Priest did manage to break away and set up Bennett, whose powerful shot was well saved by Williams, but the Albion 'keeper and his defenders were putting constant pressure on the United defence by clearing the ball high and long, with the assistance of the strong wind. While Needham was having a good game, Howell, already outpaced by Garfield in the first half, and Logan were struggling badly against the home side's forwards.

In control, Albion went two goals up. Williams played in Garfield whose hard, low shot was excellently saved by Foulke – diving at full length – but unfortunately he could only parry the ball to Richards, who knocked it into the net. Pushing on, the Albion forwards kept Foulke busy for the rest of the game but could not breakthrough again. The match ended in a fierce hailstorm.

Assessment

There could be no arguments over the result; clearly the better side had won and had adapted far more effectively to the difficult conditions. There were some positives for United. Foulke, Bennett and Priest had all played well again and Hedley, who was from South Bank where he had played with Gaudie, had passed smartly, kept his head, had an eye for goal and appeared a fit, strong player. In the team's defence they had badly missed Morren, as they had at Sunderland, and were going to play Gaudie at centre-half, but as the player was not fit when the team reached West Brom, there was no alternative but to press Logan, the only available player, into the position. Not surprisingly, Logan, a centre-forward, had proved a disaster at centre-half in such difficult conditions.

There were two major concerns over the performance, however. Firstly, United had not looked like scoring and there was a need for more potency among the inside-forwards. In addition, Howell seemed to have lost his old reliability. There had been concerns over his performance at Sunderland, and at West Brom he had 'worked very hard, yet scarcely with his old judgement'. ('Looker On', *Telegraph*, 28 February 1898) With Johnson having deputised effectively in the half-back line, the football committee made the decision to sell Howell to Liverpool – the player also had a reputation for being 'difficult' – and he had played his last game for United.

Table

		P	W	L	D	Pts
1.	United	27	14	5	8	36
2.	Sunderland	26	15	6	5	35
3.	West Brom	25	11	5	9	31
4.	Wednesday	27	14	10	3	31

Other results

Stoke 2–1 Wednesday

MATCH NO. 28

SUNDERLAND, HOME, 2 APRIL 1898

Result: United 1: *Johnson*
                  Sunderland 0

Half-time: 0–0
Attendance: 23,000

Teams:

United: Foulke, Thickett, Cain, Johnson, Morren, Howard, Bennett, Cunningham, Hedley, Almond, Priest.

Sunderland: Doig, McNeill, Boyle, Ferguson, McAlister, Dunlop, Morgan, Leslie, Brown, Wilson, Saxton.

Referee: Mr G.H. Dale (Manchester)

The period leading up to the game was full of controversy and it was centred on the line ups for both sides. The game was scheduled for the same Saturday as the England–Scotland fixture in Glasgow and as a result United had written to the Sunderland committee asking for a re-arrangement of the match, given that Needham and Thickett would probably be called-up by England, while Sunderland's Doig and Wilson would be representing Scotland. As these were key players for both teams, United argued that all should be present for what amounted to a Championship decider. United had written to Sunderland on 16 March but received no reply until the 24th. That response was to create a furore in the football world – Sunderland being roundly condemned on all sides for their unsporting attitude.

Basically Sunderland declined to move the fixture and, furthermore, it soon emerged that their players would take advantage of the fact that they would not be forced by the Scottish FA to represent their country; while United's men, if selected, would be expected to play for England by the FA's international committee. Pursuing the matter, a slight to their nation, the newspaper *Scottish Sport* elicited the

SHEFFIELD UNITED.

RIGHT WING.   *Goal :*   LEFT WING.

Foulkes.

Backs :

Thickett.   **Cain.**

Half-Backs :

Johnson.   **Morren.**   **Howard.**

Forwards :

Bennett.   **Cunningham.**   **Hedley.**   **Almond.**   **Priest.**

Referee :—Mr. G. H. DALE, of Manchester.

Forwards :

Saxton.   **Wilson.**   **Brown.**   **Leslie.**   **Morgan.**

Half-Backs :

Dunlop.   **McAlister.**   **Ferguson.**

Backs :

Boyle.   **McNeill.**

Goal :

Doig.

LEFT WING.   RIGHT WING.

SUNDERLAND.

Top and second in the table meet in this vital match, with Sunderland still having a game in hand.

following statement from the Sunderland secretary Mr R. Campbell: 'While they [Doig and Wilson] would like to play for Scotland, they would not like to do so if their absence would be the means of their own club suffering defeat. We have no capable reserves and could do nothing else but ask out players to assist us at Sheffield.'

Campbell then launched into an attack on United: 'I have only to add that if it had not been for Sheffield United insisting upon their appeal against our previous match, in addition to making strenuous efforts to secure the services of several Corinthians to oppose us, I am confident that my directors would gladly have agreed to a postponement.'

It was true that United, having played the Corinthians in the Charity Shield, had been offered the use of some of their amateur players. However, United had not requested the use of any until after receiving Sunderland's refusal to alter the fixture on 25 March and then were only really interested in getting G.O. Smith, who was unavailable as he too was picked to play for England, while Corinthians were not too keen to loan any other players. The attitude of Sunderland and their players was contrasted to that of Ernest Needham who formally asked the selection committee to leave him out of their considerations so that he could help out his club. However, once selected he dutifully accepted he would have to turn out for his country.

United thus lined up without their captain, but fortunately Morren, who would have joined him in Glasgow, was injured at the time of selection and so not called-up. With McKay absent, Hedley was kept at centre-forward, while Cunningham was switched to the inside-right position to bring Almond in at inside-left. Johnson was now in for the departed Howell, while Howard deputised for Needham. Crucially, Morren was fit again to provide experience to the half-back line. Sunderland, Doig and Wilson in the side, were at full strength.

The season had seemingly come down to this one game and the pressure had been building for some time on United. The match programme highlighted the ongoing problems: 'The records of the past few weeks are not such as to cause satisfaction to the supporters of the club. In the League we have not gained a victory since Bolton Wanders were here weeks and weeks ago.'

As a consequence, the committee had attempted to being in player reinforcements – a reference to discussions with Corinthians – but 'Our effort has failed, and we have to end the season without men as best we may.'

The club were intent on rallying all United followers to the cause and boldly declared 'We are full of confidence that those men will show us the form which proved so irresistible in January, and which beat the Villa and made us the proudest club in Britain…every man today has declared his intention of doing his very best. The errors of the past are to be wiped out.'

Facing adversity, the club indeed seemed to pull together. Nationally, sentiment was all on United's side, it being hoped that the unsporting attitude of Sunderland would be rewarded with a defeat. A crowd of 23,000, providing receipts of £540 7s 10d, attended and there was to be nothing other than fanatical support for the United team.

First half

Cain, captain in Needham's absence and making his 100th consecutive appearance, lost the toss, and Wilson, Sunderland's leader, decided to kick towards Shoreham Street with a fairly strong wind behind them.

Both sides started the game with real intent. United had the first good chance. Hedley and Bennett combined well and Boyle was forced to concede a corner on the United right. From the resultant kick, the ball fell to Bennett whose shot was well saved by Doig. Responding, Sunderland advanced the ball down the right wing, the move ending with a fine shot by Leslie which was well saved by Foulke. The game was now end to end with both sides pressing but neither able to open their account.

Johnson then produced an excellent shot which had Doig scrambling across his goal to save. Unable to gather the ball in, Sunderland's 'keeper found himself at the centre of a mass scrimmage of players, Boyle eventually managing to clear the danger. 'Bennett a minute or two afterwards raised enthusiasm to fever heat by a neck and neck race down the touch line. In spite of the fact that he was closely hugged by three Sunderland men he kept the ball at his toes, and put in a beautiful centre…shots being sent in by Priest, Cunningham and Hedley,' in the resulting melee, without success. (*Telegraph*, 4 April 1898) Sunderland responded with good shots from Saxton and Wilson, both well saved by Foulke.

For the last period of the half, though, United were well on top, taking up 'a temporary residence in the Sunderland quarters.' Unfortunately, they were unable to break the deadlock.

Second half

United now had the wind in their favour and soon began to dominate, although their shooting was a little wayward until Bennett sent a terrific strike whistling just past the post. The Sunderland goal now underwent a period of severe bombardment, the visitors hardly able to get out of their own half during the opening 15 minutes.

As the game progressed the United pressure continued, the home crowd roused to a heady pitch of excitement in the expectation that their heroes must surely score. Johnson, advancing, hit an unstoppable shot which unfortunately skimmed the top of the crossbar. After 25 minutes Sunderland finally ventured over the halfway line, Morgan initiating an attack which was quickly turned back. Almond then sent in another fierce shot, well saved by Doig. With about 13 minutes to go, United gained a corner. Played in by Priest, the ball landed in the area, causing a scramble between the two sets of players. The ball broke loose and fell to Johnson, who drilled it through a crowd of players and into the corner of the net, and 'the home supporters almost went wild with delight, and the sense of enthusiasm displayed has probably never before been equalled on the Bramall Lane ground'.

The next three minutes saw United gain two more corners without any result, and then finally Morgan got away and put a fine cross into the United area – only for Foulke to take the ball with ease. It was only the second time that the United 'keeper had touched the ball in the half, a mark of United's dominance. As the whistle went to end the game, the home side were still attacking and ran out worthy winners 1–0.

Assessment

The team had risen magnificently to the importance of the occasion, and all the players had been impressive and were clearly determined to win the game – 'they seemed to be imbued with the idea that it was a matter of life and death, and all through they played with a determination delightful to see'. ('Looker On', *Telegraph*, 4 April 1898)

The star of the show was not a United man though. Doig, the Sunderland 'keeper, had been magnificent, at times almost single-handedly denying the United team. 'We have seen some marvellous exhibitions of goalkeeping in our experience, but few, if any, came up to Doig's performance.' (*Telegraph*, 4 April 1898) It was generally acknowledged that United would have scored many more goals if the Sunderland 'keeper had turned out for Scotland.

A typical national assessment of the game came from the *Sunday Telegraph*: 'United by their victory over Sunderland have once more become first favourites for the Championship…it may be said at once that United gave probably the most brilliant exposition of the game that has been seen on the Bramall Lane ground this year. Of the United men it would be difficult to speak individually, the whole team working together with a machine-like regularity which spelt victory from the outset. Johnson was decidedly one of the best men on the field and well deserved the honour of scoring the only goal. Cain and Thickett were like a stonewall in defence, while we have never seen the United forward line in better trim. On Saturday's form the chances of the Championship coming to Sheffield are on the up-grade.'

Clearly United now had the whip hand in the title race, but there were still two games to go, and to be completely safe United had to win them both.

Table

		P	W	L	D	Pts
1.	United	28	15	5	8	38
2.	Sunderland	27	15	7	5	35
3.	West Brom	26	11	6	9	31
4.	Wednesday	27	14	10	3	31
5.	Villa	27	13	9	5	31
6.	Everton	27	11	7	9	31

Other results

Bolton 2–0 West Brom

Aston Villa 1–1 Stoke

Everton 2–0 Nottingham Forest

MATCH NO. 29

BOLTON, AWAY, 8 APRIL 1898

Result:　　Bolton 0

United 1: *Needham*

Half-time:　0–1

Attendance: 19,395, Burnden Park, receipts £523

Teams:

Bolton:　　Sutcliffe, Somerville, Davies, Fitchett, Brown, Freebairn, Thompson, Gilligan, Cassidy, Nicol, Gregory.

United:　　Foulke, Thickett, Cain, Johnson, Morren, Howard, Bennett, Needham, Almond, Cunningham, Priest.

Referee:　　Mr J. West (Lincoln)

Given this was a fixture of extraordinary importance to the club, United's football committee showed themselves perhaps too honourable, unlike their Sunderland rivals, in sending the team to London during the week to replay the Charity Shield fixture against Corinthians. Having had a tough game against Sunderland on Saturday, the team was down in London for a tough match on Monday and then had to fulfil the fixture in Bolton on Good Friday. All United's line up in the latter game, except Howard, had played three games in a week (Needham had represented England) and had been involved in a large amount of travelling. The game in London had also proved frustrating for the United players, who felt that the referee had been unduly biased towards the amateurs, ensuring the score remained 1–1 at full-time, after allowing a twice taken free-kick to give Corinthians their equaliser. Rather more sensible than their committee, the United players then refused to play extra-time, supported by the United chairman Charles Stokes, on the grounds that they had an important commitment at Bolton on Friday. As a result, the first ever Charity Shield was shared between the clubs. Sheriff Dewar, who had initiated the trophy and new annual game, commended United for 'grand sportsmanship and character' and for again playing 'for bare expenses.' It was to be hoped, however, that United's generosity had not brought the club an excellent national reputation at the expense of defeat in the title race.

When United arrived at Bolton for the Good Friday fixture, they were forced to reshuffle the side. Hedley did not turn up, as an amateur his employer refused to release him, and with Gaudie not quite fit Needham moved to inside-right to partner Bennett, and Howard remained in the half-back line. Cunningham switched back to inside-left from the right, where he had played against Sunderland. Bolton, having beaten third-placed West Brom the previous week, would be no pushover. With expectations for the title high, a special train excursion by the Great Central Line brought around 800 United supporters to Burnden Park 'including a large contingent from Staveley and neighbourhood,' who were presumably connected to Ernest Needham. (West Brom programme, 11 April 1898) Departing early, the supporters arrived well before the team, giving them time to spend in the Lancashire mill town: 'for once Bolton was beautiful, for it was fine weather, and we made quite a brave show as we kept the streets alive after the train rolled in.' The hope was that the carnival atmosphere would still be present at the final whistle.

First half
Somerville won the toss for Bolton, who played with the wind behind them. Both sides immediately announced their attacking intentions. United put together a couple of good moves – a testing Bennett cross cleared by Davies and then the same player just failed to finish off fine work by Almond and Cunningham on the left. Bad luck then hit the visitors, as a scramble in the Bolton area led to Priest being injured and forced to retire from the field. The left-winger's absence was a signal for Bolton to launch their best attack so far. From a throw in, Gregory got clear away down the left and delivered a cross which Cassidy blasted just wide.

Fortunately Priest, though clearly limping, was able to return to the fray and after 25 minutes United went a goal up. Needham worked his way out to the left, dribbled right through the Bolton defence and advanced on Sutcliffe. Expecting a fierce shot, Sutcliffe dived for the ball, only for Needham to stroke it past the committed 'keeper, whose momentum took him into a collision with the United man. With Needham landing on top of his opponent, the result was that Sutcliffe was slightly winded.

A minute later R.N. Brown, the old Wednesday player, miskicked the ball, wrenching his knee in the process, meaning he had to go off for treatment. Although he returned, like Priest he was fairly lame, so evening the sides up – although Priest went off again before half-time. There was some Bolton pressure before the interval, Foulke dealing well with a couple of corners, but United came closest to scoring again, as Needham fed Bennett and Sutcliffe brought off a good save.

Second half

Both Priest and Brown were present as the teams kicked-off, but shortly after the Bolton man had to retire. It was United who took the initiative and created the better chances during the half, although the home side did remain dangerous.

The first good chance came to United, a fiercely struck Cain free-kick well saved by Sutcliffe. Bolton then responded, a pass by Gregory released Thompson but Foulke rushed out of goal and saved. Sutcliffe then kept out shots from Howard, Needham and Cunningham. Play was now fast and furious, the referee permitting some rough challenges on both sides. Near the end Needham thought he had scored his second, but Sutcliffe expertly tipped the ball over the bar.

With the game over, Needham made his way to the Bolton secretary's office where he borrowed the telephone to find out the result of Sunderland's game at Bury. With the Wearsiders being down to nine men by half-time, they had eventually gone down to a 1–0 defeat, meaning they could no longer catch their Sheffield rivals. As Needham returned with the news to United's changing room, a rousing cheer went up from all present. United were champions!

Assessment

United had won the game comfortably, but the players had definitely suffered from the exertions of the last week. Reflecting on the victory, the United programme for the final game against West Brom declared 'a glorious day but not a glorious game…they are stiff and sore all over [the players] are tired – or were – and our trainer, rare old George Waller, has had his hands full ever since.'

It did not really matter that the game had not been an excellent one; for once the result was all-important. In its editorial comment of 9 April, the *Sheffield and Rotherham Independent* proudly wrote 'United deserve the heartiest congratulation on their success, and on the honour they have brought to the city which has been the birthplace of Association Football.'

Table

		P	W	L	D	Pts
1.	United	29	16	5	8	40
2.	Sunderland	28	15	8	5	35
3.	Everton	28	12	7	9	33
4.	West Brom	28	11	7	10	32

Other Results

Everton 3–0 Derby

MATCH NO. 30

WEST BROM, HOME, 11 APRIL 1898

Result: United 2: *Bennett (2)*
                West Brom 0

Half-time: 1–0
Attendance: 9,000

Teams:

United: Bradshaw, Thickett, Cain, Johnson, Morren, Howard, Bennett, Cunningham, Gaudie, Almond, Needham.

West Brom: Reader, Cave, Williams, Perry, Jones, Banks, Bassett, Flewitt, Richards, McKenzie, Garfield.

Referee: Unknown

Foulke and Thickett had played for the English against the Scottish League on the previous day. United's 'keeper missed his only League game of the season, Bradshaw deputising. Thickett was going to be rested too, given that he was carrying a leg injury, but Simpson of the reserves was unable to get to the ground and Thickett decided to turn out himself rather than ask French to fill in in an unfamiliar position. Unfortunately for the team, the day was exceptionally wet and this kept the crowd down to around 9,000. Nevertheless, the match programme made it clear that the players should be given a rousing reception: 'Champions we are, and our men deserve a big reception when they appear today. Give it 'em!'

The programme contained some other interesting articles. Mention was again made of the club's intention to establish an 'athletics' complex for all sports at Bramall Lane. President of the club, Michael Ellison, was thus to contact the Duke of Norfolk, who owned the ground, to try to negotiate a long lease or, more preferably, the purchase of the property. (A sale was to be finalised in February 1899.) The move was seen as a crucial one in order to keep the development of the club moving forward.

In a self-congratulatory note, it was announced that the decision to produce an official club programme had been a resounding success – it 'has more than paid its way.'

On the playing side, the club informed the supporters that, following their Charity Shield replay with Corinthians, the amateur club, conscious of how the fixture had tired the United players before their key game at Bolton, offered the services of their two key England internationals, G.O. Smith and C. Wreford-Brown. The club declared that the 'offer of men G.O. Smith and C. Wreford-Brown was generously meant, but declined because we felt it would be right to win the Championship – if it was to be won – with our own men.'

This was perhaps a strange declaration, bearing in mind the panic that had ensued over Needham's absence before the return game against Sunderland and that the club had declared, at the time, that they were interested in Corinthians offer. However, it may just have been that, following United's victory over their rivals, confidence had been restored in the abilities of all the players and the football committee were now far more relaxed in their outlook and had forgotten their previous worries.

The departure of Rab Howell to Liverpool was, quite correctly given the player's great importance to the club's success over eight seasons, marked with respect. In an article entitled 'Rab', the player was roundly commended: 'that we have parted with a real good servant in Rab Howell is known to everyone. He has been a big factor in very many of our successes in the past, and now and then we are sure to miss him. We have parted with him on good terms, and in their new half-back, Tom Watson's committee have got a still good player.'

The Match

Thickett's decision to play was taken as the teams kicked-off and United were a man down as they waited for him to get changed. This enabled the visitors to apply some pressure and Bradshaw was tested as he clawed the ball out from under the bar following a Bassett cross. Thickett, 'turning out after play had been in progress a few minutes, got a genuine cheer all to himself, and played a real good game.' (Looker On, *Telegraph*, 12 April 1898) Gaudie, filling in for Thickett, now moved up to centre-forward.

The game was competitive, with both sides making chances. Bennett was being particularly troublesome for the Albion defence, teasing left-back Williams and sending in a couple of good shots. Flewitt then forced Bradshaw into a good save, while Gaudie skimmed the top of the bar with a shot. After 20 minutes United went in front. There was a scramble in the Albion area and the ball ran to Bennett, whose low shot beat Reader 'amid a storm of cheering.' Straight away, United almost had two. Bennett got away down the right, played in to Gaudie, whose touch was cleared off the line by Reader. A cross by Needham was then headed into Reader's hands, when perhaps the forward could have done better.

United had created the better chances, in difficult conditions, yet just before half-time Albion reminded them the game was far from won; Garfield skimmed the bar, following a slick passing move by the visitors, Johnson made a last ditch interception to deny Garfield and a Bassett shot was cleared for a corner.

Second half

The continued heavy rain meant that the pitch was now treacherous and the 'players slipped about woefully.' Albion, though, were determined to get back into the match and were competing aggressively. The first real chance was United's though, as Gaudie's lightning shot was saved brilliantly by the feet of Reader. Bassett then responded with a shot that just missed the target, play then returning to the other end, as the dangerous Cunningham almost beat Reader and was then denied by a great tackle from Cave.

When United were denied a penalty by the referee for a trip by Perry on Bennett, there was frustration in the crowd, but with 11 minutes to go United did get a second. Gaudie passed to Bennett who outpaced Williams and fired past Reader 'amid a tumult of applause.' The rain was now exceptionally heavy, and although Albion pressed the home defence held firm.

Assessment

The game was academic but had turned out to be exciting despite the awful conditions. It was ironic that United, frequently condemned by the commentators for performing poorly in adverse conditions, had played so well in such circumstances in their final League game of the season. Although there had been lots of slips and tumbles, there had also been some excellent pieces of skill, most notably from Bennett. The right-winger, who 'has developed a whole body of pluck' (Looker On 12 April 1898), was ably assisted by Almond and Gaudie. Had it not been for the sturdy defensive work of Williams, 'one of England's finest backs', and Reader, United would have scored more goals.

FINAL TABLE

		P	W	D	L	F	A	W	D	L	F	A	F	A	Pts
1.	SHEFFIELD U	30	9	2	4	27	14	8	3	4	29	17	56	31	42
2	Sunderland	30	12	1	2	27	8	4	8	3	16	22	43	30	37
3	Wolverhampton W	30	10	1	4	36	14	4	8	3	21	27	57	41	35
4	Everton	30	11	1	3	33	12	2	7	6	15	27	48	39	35
5	Sheffield W	30	12	3	0	39	15	3	9	3	12	27	51	42	33
6	Aston Villa	30	12	2	1	47	21	2	9	4	14	30	61	51	33
7	West Bromwich A	30	8	2	5	25	16	3	7	5	19	29	44	45	32
8	Nottingham F	30	7	3	5	30	19	4	7	4	17	30	47	49	31
9	Liverpool	30	7	4	4	27	16	4	9	2	21	29	48	45	28
10	Derby Co	30	10	2	3	40	19	1	11	3	17	42	57	51	28
11	Bolton W	30	9	4	2	18	13	2	11	2	10	28	28	41	26
12	Preston North End	30	7	3	5	26	15	1	11	3	9	28	35	43	24
13	Notts Co	30	4	5	6	23	23	4	9	2	13	23	36	46	24
14	Bury	30	8	4	3	25	19	0	10	5	14	32	39	51	24
15	Blackburn R	30	4	4	7	20	22	3	9	3	19	32	38	54	24
16	Stoke	30	8	4	3	21	14	0	10	5	14	41	35	55	24

The Championship-winning team and committee.

FINAL NOTE

Having won the title, United were surprised to find out that the League provided no medals for the players to mark their achievement, unlike the FA who provided them for their own Cup competition. As a result, the club had their own produced and, at a victory banquet held in the Cutlers' Hall, presented them to the players, who were also given a £3 bonus – presumably in addition to those that had been accruing over the season for their match bonuses – and increased wages. Responding to a toast to the players, Needham, as captain, described his men as an honest team of 'triers.' In this he reflected the attitude of many of the national news and sporting papers of the day, as noted in the analysis of United's victory at Aston Villa. However, with a number of quality rivals to overcome, 'Nudger's' self-effacing assessment, however commendable, was indeed wide of the mark. United were a very good team, a majority would gain international honours, and they would, in the next four seasons, reach three Cup Finals, winning two, and be runners-up in the League.

A postcard showing some of the Championship-winning players and the winners' medals that the club produced.

The Colman's Mustard label showing the Championship-winning team.

BIBLIOGRAPHY

The book has been written with the aid of the following primary sources:

Newspapers
Although I have quoted from a range of local and national news and sports papers, by far the most important ones used for the coverage of the 1898–98 season are:
The Sheffield Daily Telegraph
The Sheffield and Rotherham Independent

Programmes
The Sheffield United football programme: issues for season 1897–98.

Books
Needham, Ernest, *Association Football,* is an excellent source dealing with this period of United's history and giving an insight into Nudger's own ideas on the game.
Clarebrough, Denis and Andrew Kirkham, *A Complete Record of Sheffield United Football Club 1889–1999,* provides statistical details on United's 1897–98 campaign.

The following books are useful secondary sources, and they provide the reader with a general starting point for details and statistics on United's history at the end of the 1890s.

Clarebrough, Denis *Sheffield United Football Club. The First 100 Years.*
Farnsworth, Keith *Sheffield Football. A History. Volume I 1857–1961.*
Matthews, Tony, Denis Clarebrough and Andrew Kirkham *The Official Encyclopaedia of Sheffield United.*
Young, Percy M. *Football in Sheffield.*

Printed in Germany
by Amazon Distribution
GmbH, Leipzig